I FLEW FOR THE FÜHRER

WINGS OF WAR

For the vaunted German Luftwaffe, World War II was a down-ward spiral from apparent greatness in Poland to unmitigated disaster on all fronts. *I Flew for the Führer* records the heights and depths of that epic journey in the incredible career of Heinz Knoke, a gallant and indestructible fighter pilot.

Knoke entered front-line service with the famous Fifty-Second Fighter Wing in January 1941. For the next four years he tilted against overwhelming Allied strength from German bases throughout Europe. His victims included nineteen four-engine bombers, the toughest targets in the sky.

Knoke was innovative and determined; among his more daring exploits was the first air-to-air bombing of U.S. forma-tions. Without any official authorization, Knoke armed his Messerschmitt 109 with a 500-pound bomb, which he dropped into a B-17 formation. One B-17 was destroyed and others were damaged, a triumph that earned him the personal congratulations of Reich Marshal Herman Göring.

As German strength declined, there began the usual harassment from Headquarters, trying to extract from the blood of the pilots the resources that poor planning and over-ambitious war aims had squandered. Yet it is in this latter part of the war, when he and his comrades were pitted against hundreds of American fighters, that Knoke's character and ability stand out. His daily sorties saw victories, but also endless defeats; Knoke was shot down many times, but he always came back to fight again, flying obsolete fighters against impossible odds. "The inescapable fact is that on the technical side our performance is inferior in every respect," he writes. "Such successes as are still being achieved in the face of these overwhelming odds are due simply and solely to the excellent morale and fighting spirit of our aircrews. We need more aircraft, better engines—and fewer Headquarters."

The overextended Luftwaffe kept its pilots in the line until they died. Downed pilots routinely staggered from their para-

TIME-LIFE BOOKS INC., ALEXANDRIA, VIRGINIA 22314

chute harnesses into cockpits to re-enter the fray. Only twenty-six days after bailing out of his Messerschmitt and suffering a fractured skull and vertebrae and a variety of other injuries, Knoke hobbled on crutches out to his fighter to accompany his Flight to a new assignment in Holland. He was immediately shot down by intercepting Spitfires.

In the end, it was usually only a serious but nonfatal wound that permitted a Luftwaffe pilot to survive. Knoke suffered his in late 1944 at the hands of Czech partisans, when the car in which he was traveling struck a mine. After flying four hundred missions and serving as the youngest Squadron Commander in the German Air Force, he spent the final months of the war on the ground as an Air Liaison Officer, an ardent patriot distressed by a growing awareness of the horrors of the Nazi regime he was defending. Heinz Knoke is officially credited with thirty-three combat victories. The figure of fifty-two victories quoted in the book's foreword arose from a misinterpretation of a wartime document.

Knoke's postwar years were highlighted by successful careers in business and politics and sustained by his happy marriage to Lilo, with whom he lives in Bad Iburg, West Germany. Knoke retired from business in 1986, and is now pursuing the study of philosophy and literature.

Walter J. Boyne

Captain *(Hauptmann)* Heinz Knoke: for downing 52 enemy planes he won the coveted Knight's Cross and the Nazi's German Gold Cross.

I FLEW FOR THE FÜHRER

The Story of a German Fighter Pilot

BY

HEINZ KNOKE

Translated by
John Ewing

With an Introduction by
Lieutenant General E. R. Quesada
United States Air Force (ret.)

ILLUSTRATED WITH PHOTOGRAPHS

HENRY HOLT AND COMPANY
NEW YORK

Introduction

Upon finishing this airman's story, I unconsciously returned to his first page and was struck with the apt irony that Knoke should have been born in Hamelin. He writes, "Most people know the story of the Pied Piper," but he did not go on to say that in a very real sense he himself re-enacted that famous fable in his own life span. As the children of Hamelin followed the fascinating music of the Pied Piper and disappeared forever into a mountain cavern, so did young Knoke follow the music of another piper, Adolf Hitler, and to the brink of his own destruction.

This young boy was very much like "the boy next door" or "the kid around the corner" who went off to war for the U.S.A. He was pliable. He was intrigued by the romance of war and he had a deep and genuine love for his homeland. He cannot be blamed for having been born a German. He was a fine airman, very brave, and an excellent pilot. I would have liked having him in one of my own squadrons had he been from a different mold.

But Knoke was betrayed by his leaders. At the beginning of the last war the German General Staff was considered by the students of military history to consist of military geniuses. Leadership, however, was in the hands of a sinister group whose motives were based on false values and lacked philosophical morality. It eventually contaminated the war machine. This pollution became especially apparent in defeat, and the effects are evident as Knoke finishes his story describing military and political leadership as hysterical and impractical.

Some details of this volume seem exaggerated to me. (Our own pilots could also, on occasion, do some fancy fact-stretching.) For example, I do not believe, as Knoke does, that any German ace shot down 150 Allied planes. Here and there his book contains other statements which I regard as obvious Nazi propaganda, swallowed whole by an eager youth. But in the main, the diary forms a solid and truthful picture of one man's war, often brutal, sometimes desperate, and always courageous.

Knoke's bitter hatred of Russia is significant, for he found in Soviet leadership the same lack of moral fiber that he finally recognized in the Nazi regime.

But in the beginning he did not see these weaknesses. He was just a typical German boy being misled. Note especially the entry for December 18, 1940, when he writes of the ceremony in the Berlin Sportpalast when he first saw Hitler: "Some minutes pass. Then, at an order, we spring up smartly to attention. 'Here comes the Führer!' . . . Absolute silence reigns in the vast hall. . . . Then Hitler begins to speak. I do not suppose that the world has ever known a more brilliant orator than this man. His magnetic personality is irresistible. One can sense the emanations of tremendous will power and driving energy."

I am reminded of Robert Browning's lines in the *Pied Piper of Hamelin:*

> All the little boys and girls,
> With rosy cheeks and flaxen curls,
>
> .   .   .   .   .
>
> Tripping and skipping, ran merrily after
> The wonderful music with shouting and laughter.

It is an appropriate coincidence that Knoke should have been a youth from Hamelin.

LIEUTENANT GENERAL E. R. QUESADA
United States Air Force (ret.)

I FLEW FOR THE FÜHRER

1

The Early Years

Most people know the story of the Pied Piper of Hamelin.

The road in Hamelin which was followed by the children who were on their way to the mountain of Koppenberg, never more to return, is still known to this day as the Koppenstrasse. There are houses along it now, ugly and gray, with narrow, dingy courtyards. The rough road surface is a dust trap in summer. It is a mass of potholes, which in the spring and autumn rains become large, deep puddles. It has not yet been paved and finishes by dwindling into a footpath to the fields and vegetable gardens at the foot of the Koppenberg.

My early years were spent on that road. It was not an attractive road; but, then, I was not an attractive child. I was all red hair and freckles.

My father was a policeman. During the First World War he was a Staff Sergeant in No. 10 Company, 18th Infantry Regiment. He was an impressive-looking man and a fine soldier. Afterward he served for many years on the city police force, admired and respected by his fellow citizens. He won a decoration in the Battle of Flanders, but was captured outside Ypres in 1915. He spent four long years as a prisoner of war in the island camp on Belle Île in the Bay of Biscay. He returned in 1919 and married. Anna was the most attractive of the daughters of the carpenter and bricklayer, Wilhelm Maertens. From her father she inherited her pigheadedness and also a grand sense of humor. Even now, her eyes can still gaily illuminate her smooth, unlined features beneath the white hair. I always felt that my father showed his good taste in marrying Anna, and that I would have done the same in his place.

I was born one year and eight days after the marriage of my parents, on March 24, 1921. I was far from being an ideal child. My father had to bring me up the hard way. He saw to it that at an early age I became accustomed to the Prussian conception of order and discipline. His principal aid to education was a long leather strap, with which my backside became painfully well acquainted. The Staff Sergeant treated me like a very new recruit. Yet I know that he loved me, and I am grateful to him now—even for the hidings. I must admit that they were richly deserved.

For a playground I had the barracks. There were the big parade ground and stables, and living quarters with long corridors and halls. At an early age I knew how to use a rifle, cleaning, aiming, and firing it, also how to set up a machine gun in position. I was never frightened by the noise of shooting. The soldiers were my friends and playmates: we had some great times together.

The years rolled on. It was rare for anything much in the way of excitement to disturb the peace and calm of life in our town. It rested as it had always rested there, at the foot of gentle slopes of tree-covered hills. The river still flowed past, swirling and tumbling over two wide weirs, a part of it diverted to provide power for the big flour mill on the island. Tugs battled against the current, with long strings of barges in tow. Unwieldy rafts and heavily loaded barges sailed and drifted down the valley, past the long quays and tidy promenades on the river bank. The summers brought large numbers of tourists by car and motor coach. The atmosphere of medieval romance about the old city was a big attraction and brought plenty of business to hotels, restaurants, shops, and tourist guides, especially on fine Sundays.

That was where I grew up, happy and carefree as a boy.

By 1931 I had completed four years elementary schooling and became a pupil at the high school *(Gymnasium)*. This was an ancient establishment, steeped in tradition. I came to love the old school and all that it stood for. Not that I was ever a star pupil, any more than I had been a little angel as a child. Of course, I committed every crime in the school calendar, and I suppose I was a perfect nuisance to my teachers. They seemed to take my bad behavior for granted, however, for they bore me no lasting ill will.

I shall never forget the senior tutor, old Dr. Trobitius, a most remarkable man. It was a pity that he taught mathematics, chemistry, and biology. The only subjects that interested me were philosophy, languages, history, and art. Also I was very keen on sports, especially rowing, and in the summer of 1937 I became captain of the school Rowing Club. Everyone in my class also took dancing lessons. There was very little time to spare for study. On general principles, therefore, I made it a practice never to attend any of the biology or chemistry classes. I got away with it, too, for nearly six months; but the authorities eventually caught up with me. I was faced with the prospect of expulsion from the school.

I was called up in front of the headmaster. As far as we were concerned, he was the complete personification of

Authority, a tall, lean man with scholarly features, immaculate in appearance, a Lieutenant Colonel in the Reserves.

He sat behind his great desk, smoking an acrid Virginia cigar. Beside him in an easy chair slumped Trobitius with his shiny bald pate. They both ignored me completely. I felt very uneasy. My conscience was troubled. Perhaps I had not been quite so clever as I had imagined.

Why had I been cutting the classes of Dr. Trobitius? the headmaster finally inquired.

I might have tried some excuse, such as a sore throat or a bellyache, or another stand-by of that kind. This time, however, I decided to tell the truth. I am certainly not the sort who believes fanatically in telling the truth at all times, but I thought it might be a good idea to do so then. I did not want to feel ashamed of having told lies when up in front of the headmaster. Furthermore, I reasoned that the truth could make a good impression and thus reduce the severity of my punishment.

I told the headmaster quite frankly that I was not interested in classes taught by Dr. Trobitius; that he made them too dry and boring. At that, of course, Trobitius nearly had a fit. The headmaster looked at me in astonishment; he had been waiting for one of the usual excuses. Then he thundered away at me for several minutes. But the lightning was reserved for poor old Trobitius, after I had been dismissed from their presence.

I was not punished. Classes of Dr. Trobitius after that seemed to become more interesting. . . .

That same summer at dancing class I fell in love for the first time. I adored her with all the romantic ardor of my sixteen years. Her name was Lieselotte, and her father was a doctor. Her mother, a lady of the upper classes, had no use for me because my father was only a common policeman.

About that time, too, I first started to write. I was fortunate enough to be able to sell some short stories and articles. They brought in some welcome pocket money. I also wrote some little poems for Lieselotte. She was delighted with them.

The following year I was madly in love with Annaliese. She had the figure of a goddess. I presented her with the same poems. All I had to do was alter the name: they made her just as happy.

To both Lieselotte and Annaliese I swore eternal devotion. After becoming an airman, however, I broke all the promises I had ever made them. I am still glad that my straight red hair and the freckles on my nose did not prevent them from loving me.

Apart from Lieselotte and Annaliese, my love in those days was for the old school, our town with its quaint corners and narrow streets, the boating on the river. My true love then was life itself.

In 1931 I joined the Association of Boy Scouts *(Pfadfinderbund)*. We used to roam all over Germany, camping and hiking, developing a feeling of comradeship in sing-songs round the campfire.

On January 30, 1933, when the Nazis came into power, I was 12 years of age. I remember the day perfectly. At noon the Storm Troopers *(SA)* took over the city hall and ran up the swastika flag. My father happened to be on duty in the building at the time. He and two other police officers hauled the flag down again. That incident was held against him for many years.

A few weeks later a special church service was held one Sunday for the various youth organizations. I was one of the scouts who attended. Coming out of the church into the market square, we were set upon by members of the Hitler

Youth *(HJ)*, and a violent street fight ensued. The police had to intervene.

At Whitsun a Boy Scout Jamboree was held on Lüneburg Heath, with 20,000 boys under canvas. Hitler Youths tried to wreck our camp. We fought them off, and they were soundly beaten. The Jamboree was banned in consequence, by order of the Minister of the Interior, and the camp had to be dispersed within a few hours. The Association of Boy Scouts was declared an illegal organization; and we were all collectively incorporated into the German Young Folk *(Jungfolk)*, a junior division of the Hitler Youth. We former scouts stayed together, and formed a troop *(Fahnlein)*, and continued with our hikes and camps and sing-songs as before.

In 1935, when I was 14, I became eligible for transfer into the Hitler Youth proper. I refused the opportunity. Two years later, however, I yielded to the pressure and joined the Mechanized Hitler Youth. I was very soon in trouble with the authorities. As captain of the school Rowing Club I was generally considered to be something of a reactionary in my ideas. There was an incident after a boat race at a regatta, when some club members again became involved in a fight with the Hitler Youth *Streifendienst*, a kind of boys' police force. In order to avoid the disgrace of expulsion from the Hitler Youth, I rejoined the Young Folk. There I took over the organization and supervision of sports and camps for the boys, and thus I was able to keep drill and regimentation at a minimum, placing the emphasis on freedom and good fun and fellowship.

The Hitler Youth was like every other Nazi organization. It eventually became intolerable, because of failure to apply correctly in practice the fundamental principles of National Socialism. It must be remembered, however, that the fundamental principles and ideals appealed very strongly to young people. We supported those ideals with unqualified enthusiasm, and we were able to take a real pride in the powerful resurgence of our beloved country during the years when we were young.

July 6, 1938, was the day when I went up for my first flight. It was during an air display, when an old transport aircraft was taking off from a large field outside the city. A 15-minute joy ride cost only a few marks.

Late that afternoon I sat strapped in a chair inside the body of the clumsy-looking plane. They started up the engine. The aircraft waddled awkwardly across the end of the bumpy field, where it turned into the wind. The engine roared, there were two or three bumps, and then the grass fell away beneath us. I was flying.

We climbed. Opposite my chair there was a little box, marked "Airsickness." It contained a few paper bags. I wondered why. There was no rolling, no air pockets, no motion except the gentle vibration of the chair. Higher and higher we climbed. From the air my home town looked ridiculously small. Soon we were above the level of the surrounding hilltops. The broadening horizon faded into haze. The fields diminished in size and blended into a ground mosaic of little geometrical figures, with colors ranging from dark green in the river-side meadows to bright yellow in the mustard fields, a landscape intersected by roads and railways and the winding silver ribbon of the river, varied by little toy towns and villages with red and black rooftops, and by the forests and grassy clearings on the hills, the entire picture a medley of gloriously assorted colors. Here were tiny specks on the roads which were cars or carts, or if on the river they were barges or rafts. There a miniature train, crawling along the railway track like a little black worm.

When we turned, it appeared as if the picture in all its

glory had tilted up like the top of a table. I looked at the clouds. They were quite close. "Come on," I thought, "let's get up above them!" That was when I decided that I was going to fly above the clouds one day. I was disappointed to notice that we had already begun to lose altitude. The ground came up to meet us; and soon, far too soon, it was all over.

I was still flushed with excitement when I told my parents about my first flight. They laughed. Years later I noticed the same smile on their faces when, as a veteran pilot, I told them something of the 2,000 and more flights which then lay behind me. Perhaps there was also the same flush of excitement on my own face, even then.

Summer, 1939

Summer is the climax of the year. I am by nature inclined to reckon the years of my life by the summers. Summer, with warm, sunny days and gently whispering nights.

The year 1939 is eventful for Germany and decisively affects the lives of the German people. The summer marks the end of the happy and carefree days of my youth. Once again I roam the beech and pine forests on the mountains, or the fertile cornfields and meadows of the valley. Once again I drift lazily down the River Weser in a collapsible canoe.

Annaliese shares this loveliest of all summers with me. Together we stroll through the cloisters of the Möllenbeck monastery and listen to the organ playing in the old abbey at Fischbeck. We are suntanned as we motorcycle in the Teutoburg Forest, or up the Exter Valley to the Solling. Together we scramble up the cliffs of the Hohenstein or swim in the cool water of the Weser.

We pay no attention to the storm clouds gathering on the

political horizon. What difference can it make to our lives, even though the international tension in Europe should reach breaking point? Recent years have seen Germany ridding herself more and more of the shackles of the Treaty of Versailles. Do we not have a right to live as a free people upon this earth?

Want, poverty, unemployment? They have ceased to exist in the Third Reich. Is it so strange, therefore, for Austria to have sought union with a strong and prosperous Reich? It seems only common sense for the people of the Sudeten territory to do the same, and for Memel to seek freedom from Lithuanian rule.

German populations all over Europe are reaching hands out to Hitler. It is the same wherever we go. At the National Party Rally at Nürnberg, or at the local village harvest festivals on the Bückeburg, only five miles from Hamelin, I am only one out of many millions of enthusiastic young people who have absolute faith in Hitler and dedicate themselves to him without reservations.

Annaliese and I enjoy a carefree summer, untroubled by storm clouds on the horizon. "No need to worry: the Führer will see us through," we echo the thoughts of 90 million Germans all over the world.

At the beginning of the summer I make application for service in the Air Force (*Luftwaffe*) as an officer candidate. I want to combine a military career with the freedom and beauty of life as an airman.

On July 5, I am called up for a preliminary examination. It lasts four days. Psychologists, doctors, teachers, and officers test four other candidates and me in order to determine physical and mental aptitude for our intended career. The first day is filled with medical examinations by different specialists. The second day we have to write essays, deliver

impromptu talks, and answer hundreds of questions in tests
by officers and psychologists. The third day finds us in the
"three-dimensional chair," rotated and spun in various positions, our reactions tested by means of an elaborate system
of press buttons. We have to crawl into a low-pressure
chamber and are timed while fitting together little sets of
gears and cog wheels to determine the effect of lack of
oxygen. It seems like going through an up-to-date torture
chamber.

The fourth and last day is for tests of athletic proficiency.
They cover running, both long distance and sprinting, jump-
ing, throwing the discus and javelin, gymnastics on single
and horizontal parallel bars, swimming, and boxing. It is the
most exacting and comprehensive examination I have had in
my whole life.

In the evening we learn the results. Two candidates are
successful. I am one of them.

August 27, 1939

Our school becomes a barracks overnight, and the Armed
Forces call up the Reserves. There seems to be a critical situation developing on the eastern border of Germany and in
Poland. Postmen are at work all through the night, hastening
along the streets to deliver call-up notices and telegrams.

August 28, 1939

The Reich government orders a general mobilization. We
are on the brink of war.

At our old school a Reserve Battalion is in process of formation. It is the same at every other school in town. The two
Army depots have overflowed, and there is field gray everywhere. The town is full of soldiers.

August 29, 1939

I am informed that I may expect my call-up from the Air Force to be accelerated. My classmates are joining up as volunteers. By evening they are already in uniform.

August 30, 1939

The leader of the local Young Folk organization *(Jung-bann)* has been called up. I take over the command of about 4,000 boys in the Hamelin District *(Kreis)*. They have to be posted everywhere, to help the soldiers and make themselves generally useful. At supply depots there are requisitioned vehicles to be loaded with stores and equipment, arms and ammunition; in the barracks there are many ways to help; in field kitchens there are potatoes to be peeled, etc. Wherever there are soldiers the boys are sent to help.

In the afternoon the first of our newly mobilized battalions is entrained at the freight depot. Trains are decorated with flowers as they leave for the east, but the faces are solemn. I recognize some of my classmates among them. The grim steel helmets contrast sharply against the youthful faces. *(Most of them I never see again.)*

August 31, 1939

The Polish atrocities against the German minority make horrible reading today. Thousands of Germans are being massacred daily in territory which had once been part of Germany. Thousands more arrive every hour in the Reich, each refugee with another tale of horror.

September 1, 1939

At 0540 hours this morning the German armies move across the border into action. That means war.

Thus ends the last summer of my boyhood. Thus a humble, insignificant individual is caught in the relentless path of the giant wheel of Time. I must be prepared for war to descend like an avalanche upon my head. I shall have to become as tough as steel, or be crushed. My most ardent desire now is to become a soldier.

September 5, 1939

On September 2, Göring called up the civil air defense services. Yesterday brought a surprising declaration of war against the German Reich by Britain and France. Today, for the first time, the wail of air-raid warning sirens is heard over Hamelin, as British bombers attack harbors and installations along the North Sea coast of Germany.

September 8, 1939

Warsaw has fallen.

The Polish campaign is a lightning war *(Blitzkrieg)*. The advance of the German armies has become an irresistible march to victory. Scenes of deep emotion occur with the liberation of the terrorized German residents of the Polish Corridor. Dreadful atrocities, crimes against all the laws of humanity, are brought to light by our armies. Near Bromberg and Torun they discover mass graves containing the bodies of thousands of Germans who have been massacred by the Polish Communists.

The Polish Army is disintegrating: the Polish Air Force has been smashed already. Here in Germany it is believed that the war will be over by Christmas. The people want peace. Sacrifice of lives is the price we have to pay for victory.

September 11, 1939

This morning my father left for active duty with a police detachment in Poland.

My sister on the North Sea island of Wangerooge experiences the first British air raids.

My mother and I are now left alone in our Hamelin home —the "Rat-hole." It is strange how quiet it is there. I, too, shall soon be gone.

The war in Poland draws to its close. Perhaps we can still look forward to a family reunion for Christmas, after all.

I apply for my call-up to be advanced, but cannot get anything definite beyond some vague promises which mean nothing. I do not know exactly why it is, but somehow the prospect of actually experiencing war rather appeals to me.

September 27, 1939

After several days of writing my senior matriculation examination *(Abitur)*, I learn today that I have passed. So now I am finished with school. Many a time in the past I have damned the old place, but I love it, nevertheless. Farewell to the familiar institute of learning; and a special farewell to good old Dr. Trobitius. He seems to have forgiven me for having cut his biology classes, and clasps my hand for a long time as he wishes me good luck in my future life as an airman. Yesterday brought news of the deaths of the first two of my classmates. Both had fallen in the Battle for Radom.

October 30, 1939

My Air Force call-up finally arrived today. I am to report on November 15 to No. 11 Flying Training Regiment at Schönwalde near Berlin.

The war in Poland has been over for more than a month. There is comparatively little activity on our West Wall line. Only the Air Force is in action daily. I wonder if I shall ever fly on an operational mission.

November 13, 1939

Days drag slowly into weeks, and I am bursting with impatience. Only two more days, and I shall be a soldier.

This is my last day at home. My mother does not speak of my departure. I know that things are going to be difficult for her after I am gone.

November 14, 1939

At noon today I left Hamelin. "Everything will be all right," says my mother. She and Annaliese are there to see me off, waving as the train pulls out of the station.

I spend my last night as a civilian in Berlin, and I find the noise and hustle of the great city very tiring.

November 15, 1939

At 1515 hours I enter Schönewalde Airfield, where No. 11 Flying Training Regiment is based, and report at the Orderly Room of No. 4 Company. I am now Recruit Knoke. At Clothing Stores I am issued with slacks which are too loose and a tunic which is too tight for me, a pair of incredibly heavy clodhopper boots, and a steel helmet which is much too small.

I venture a mild protest about the helmet, only to be put in my place by the Quartermaster Sergeant: "You shut your trap!" he snarls. "That helmet fits. Can I help it if you have got a swelled head?"

Since then I have been in a complete daze. All movements have to be at the double. The place is as busy as an ant heap. They all dash about the barracks, to the echo of shouted orders and hobnailed boots tramping down the long corridors and stairways—soldiers, soldiers, nothing but soldiers everywhere. This strange, unglamorous world makes me feel very lonely.

December 24, 1939

Christmas Eve. The war should have been over long ago.

It is my first Christmas away from home. There they will have snow on the ground: here we have had several days of rain. We are in the middle of basic military training, and it is really tough. There is the same grinding routine day after day: parades, drill, maneuvers, firing practice, sports, lectures, fatigue duties, inspections, etc. . . .

It is once again apparent that I am not a prodigy. Indeed, my NCO even goes so far as to say that if I am ever commissioned as an officer he will apply for discharge from the service and give up all Christmas presents for seven years. During the monotonous drill parades I like to imagine myself bashing that so-and-so over the head with a rifle butt.

I am dead tired. Tomorrow night I am on guard duty, but the following day I am allowed an extra hour in bed. That extra hour will be my best Christmas present this year.

December 26, 1939

Boxing Day. We are confined to camp. I climb over the fence because there is a girl outside who says she is looking for her brother. I make some inquiries, but cannot find him because it is after dark. We spend some hours walking together in the woods, and I kiss her. She wants to come back again to see if she can find her brother on Sunday. Perhaps I can get in some more kissing then; I should certainly like to see what she looks like in daylight. If I had been caught climbing the fence by the Orderly Sergeant or one of the guards on duty it would have meant three days in the guardhouse for me.

2

January 31, 1940

I am posted on January 8 to the Military Academy (*Kriegschule*). Life here is no picnic for officer candidates. Drill parades continue with undiminished severity in the best Prussian tradition; but I am accustomed to it by now. "Here you have got to be tough," they keep telling us, "tough as Krupps' steel. Anyone who weakens will be washed out."

Life for us is one long grind between parade ground and lecture room. We have to study and work over books in our quarters, often until late at night. We have first-class instructors, officers, NCOs, and technicians, and they pass on to us the comprehensive knowledge which they possess of such matters as combat tactics in the air and on the ground, aeronautics, engineering, gunnery, and meteorology. A junior leadership training course has also been started.

We are now waiting for the weather to become more settled, and then flying training will begin.

February 17, 1940

At 1305 hours I have my first flying lesson in a Focke-Wulf 44, a dual-control biplane trainer, identification letters TQBZ, with Van Diecken as my instructor.

February 23, 1940

Last week I made 35 flights. The ground is covered with deep snow, and so the aircraft have been equipped with skis.

The thirty-sixth flight is a test: I am with Senior Lieutenant Woll, chief flying instructor for the course. He does not think much of my flying progress.

April 1, 1940

I have completed 83 training flights. Senior Lieutenant Woll tested me again on the last two. "You certainly cannot call those landings: they were scarcely more than controlled crashes." He shakes his head.

Added to which I got into a hopeless muddle while making a circuit of the field. The crate was completely out of control, while I fumbled desperately with stick, rudder, and throttle. We were in a spin before I knew it, heading for a nearby church. Woll grasped the throttle and brought the plane back under control. Then he turned to me. "What are you trying to do—make my wife a widow? Blasted idiot!" he shouted.

I am to be given one more chance, a positively last chance, after ten more instruction flights with Van Diecken. Pupils who fail to complete the flying course at the Military Academy are posted to the Antiaircraft Command *(Flakartillerie)*. It is a grim prospect.

April 2, 1940

Sergeant Van Diecken took me up for my final ten flights today. All the other pupils on the course have flown solo long ago. Tomorrow I am to be given a final test by Senior Lieutenant Woll.

The instruction group under Van Diecken includes three

other officer candidates besides myself: Geiger, Menapace, and Hain, and the four of us share a room.

Geiger is a North German, reserved but intensely keen. His father is a common laborer. A scholarship won at an "Adolf Hitler School" gave this very intelligent boy his chance. Having obtained his senior matriculation, he is eligible to be commissioned as an officer.

Menapace and Hain are Austrian. They both came from the mountains of the Tyrol. Sepp Menapace is the best of us at flying. He seems to do it instinctively. Short and dark and very wiry, he is a true outdoor type. He may be rather shy and awkward socially, and on the ground the movements of his muscular body may seem clumsy, like those of an automaton; but once in the air he is at home, moving as sensitively as a cat. His natural aptitude enables him to handle the controls as if he had been doing it all his life.

Hain went solo after his fortieth training flight with Van Diecken. The three of them have been watching my last few landings, and encourage me. Even Geiger opens his mouth to say merely: "You are going to be all right."

April 3, 1940

At precisely 1300 hours I take off for my first solo.

"When you come in to land, it is better to flatten out ten feet too high than one foot too low underground." Senior Lieutenant Woll shouts this parting word of advice above the roar of the engine, and grins sardonically as he steps back.

I tighten the safety belt. Throttle open gently, start moving forward, ease the stick forward as speed increases. TQBZ practically takes off by itself, and I am climbing before I am over the end of the runway.

Red streamers flutter from the wing tips, a warning to all

whom it may concern: "Careful! This is a pupil on first solo. Keep clear if you value your life."

For several minutes I circle the field. The tension gradually disappears, and I begin to relax. It is not necessary to make such efforts to keep the aircraft under control. I glance downward and watch the cloud shadows scudding across the ground. I am really flying now, free as a bird.

It is time to land. I start gliding, and the ground comes up to meet me. Throttle back, flatten out, gently now, and— bump! I am back on terra firma, and somehow the aircraft is still in one piece.

My first solo landing cannot be described as a good one. Nor were the next four I made much better. But at least the wheels did not come off.

May 10, 1940

Our armies on the West Wall start the great offensive against France, but I am afraid that I am going to be too late to see any action.

May 16, 1940

Several weeks of settled good weather have enabled us to make real progress with our training. I have completed nearly 250 flights. Now we are being taught aerobatics in the F-W 44 and the Bücker Jungmann. We also learn to fly operational aircraft, obsolete interceptor and short-range reconnaissance types like the Arado 65 and 68 and the Heinkel 45 and 46. We use the Junkers W 34 in which Kohl and Hünefeld once flew the Atlantic, and a specially adapted Focke-Wulf Weihe for long-range cross-country navigation work.

Yesterday I was on a flight to East Prussia in a rickety old crate of a GO 145, when the engine failed. The main fuel line had broken. I was only a few hundred feet up at the time, and there was not much chance of finding an emergency field for a forced landing. I came down in a plowed field. The undercarriage sheared off, the plane overturned, and I crawled out from under with a cut head.

I had to return by train. There is a fat bandage round my head. People on the platform look at me, evidently assuming that I must have been wounded in the fighting in France. It is embarrassing to admit that I have only fallen on my nose.

May 19, 1940

I seem to have struck a patch of bad luck. Today my undercarriage came off as I was trying to land at Altdamm. A very strong gale was blowing at the time, and it turned out to be too strong for the old KL 35.

Once again I have to return by train.

August 16, 1940

I now have my certificate as a pilot, and the period of flying training is over.

On June 1, I was promoted to Corporal.

The war meanwhile continues. France surrendered in June. The French could not do much against the superb morale and up-to-date equipment of the German armies. They had to use armaments which had been obsolete for a long time; indeed, some of their heavy artillery had been used in the First World War.

The British divisions apparently were kept more or less intact, although they lost vast quantities of equipment at Dunkirk. Skillful operations on the part of the British High Command enabled most of their units to return to the Island without suffering too many casualties. The German Air Force evidently lost a golden opportunity in letting them slip through our fingers at Dunkirk.

Britain does not appear to be sufficiently well armed to fight a war, and the Royal Air Force conducts its operations on a comparatively small scale. I do not understand why we did not immediately press on our advance against Great Britain: that would have meant the end of the war.

The French Air Force, too, was incapable of taking a decisive part in the fighting. Here, as in Poland, the German Air Force gave another demonstration of the overwhelming superiority of its equipment and training. This does not mean that British and French airmen lacked courage as our opponents in the air. It means that they were operating under the worst possible conditions.

The speed of the French collapse was fundamentally due, in my opinion, to poor morale in their combat divisions. *(French officers subsequently admitted as much to me with great bitterness.)* The French soldier of 1940 was not like the earlier *poilu* who fought so bravely and tenaciously in defense of every inch of his homeland during the First World War. For the last 20 years France has been resting happily on the laurels of Versailles. That is the danger of victory in any war.

The morale of the German people at home is good—perhaps rather too good!

August 26, 1940

I am to be a fighter pilot.

Posting orders came through a few days ago for Menapace and me to go to No. 1 Fighter School at Werneuchen. This afternoon we made our first operational training flight in an AR 68. The instructor is Flight Sergeant Kuhl, who had served with distinction in Poland and France. He certainly put us through it. I was feeling completely dazed and soaked in perspiration by the time we landed.

Our general military training continues. We are also given instruction in basic air-combat tactics.

The Commandant of the school is Colonel Count Huwald, who was a pilot in the famous Richtofen Wing during the First World War. The Chief Instructor is Major von Kornatzky, who was until recently Adjutant to Reich Marshal Göring. Every one of the officers and instructors is an experienced ex-operational pilot.

October 12, 1940

I had hoped for a posting to an operational unit this month. Unfortunately, training is far behind schedule because of the bad autumn weather.

We have a rough time in training here also. There have been one or two fatal accidents every week for the past six weeks in our class alone. Today Sergeant Schmidt crashed and was killed. He was one of our section of five.

We had spent several days on theoretical conversion training before flying the Messerschmitt 109, which is difficult to handle and dangerous at first. We were able to go through every movement in our sleep.

This morning we brought out the first 109 and were ready to fly. Sergeant Schmidt was chosen as the first of us by drawing lots. He took off without difficulty, which was something, as the aircraft will only too readily crash on take-off if one is not careful. A premature attempt to climb will cause it to whip over into a spin, swiftly and surely. I have seen that happen hundreds of times, and it frequently means the death of the pilot.

Schmidt came in to land after making one circuit; but he misjudged the speed, which was higher than that to which he was accustomed, and so he overshot the runway. He came round again, and the same thing happened. We began to worry, for Sergeant Schmidt had obviously lost his nerve. He was coming in and making a final turn before flattening out to touch down when the aircraft suddenly stalled because of insufficient speed and spun out of control, crashing into the ground and exploding a few hundred feet short of the end of the runway. We all raced like madmen over to the scene of the crash. I was the first to arrive. Schmidt had been thrown clear and was lying several feet away from the flaming wreckage. He was screaming like an animal, covered in blood. I stooped down over the body of my comrade and saw that both legs were missing. I held his head. The screams were driving me insane. Blood poured over my hands. I have never felt so helpless in my life. The screaming finally stopped and became an even more terrible silence. Then Kuhl and the others arrived, but by that time Schmidt was dead.

Major von Kornatzky ordered training to be resumed forthwith, and less than an hour later the next 109 was brought out. This time it was my turn.

I went into the hangar and washed the blood off my hands. Then the mechanics tightened up my safety belt, and I was taxiing over to the take-off point. My heart was madly thumping. Not even the deafening roar of the engine was loud enough to drown out of my ears the lingering screams of my comrade as he lay there dying like an animal. I was no sooner airborne than I noticed the stains on my flying suit. They were great dark bloodstains, and I was frightened. It was a horrible, paralyzing fear. I could only be thankful that there was no one else there to see how terrified I was.

I circled the field for several minutes and gradually recovered from the panic. At last I was sufficiently calm to come in for a landing. Everything was all right. I took off immediately and landed again. And a third time.

Tears were still in my eyes when I pushed open the canopy and removed my helmet. When I jumped down from the wing I found I could not control the shaking of my knees.

Suddenly I saw Kornatzky standing in front of me. Steely blue eyes seemed to be boring right through me.

"Were you frightened?"

"Yes, sir."

"Better get used to it if you hope to go on operations."

That really hurt. I was so ashamed I wished the ground would swallow me up.

October 14, 1940

This morning I was one of the six NCO officer candidates who acted as pallbearers at the funeral of Sergeant Schmidt.

Late this afternoon there was a mid-air collision over the field. Two pupils in No. 2 Flight were killed instantly. Once again I was among the first to reach the crash, and dragged one of the bodies out of the wreckage. The head was a shapeless pulp.

At this rate I shall soon become hardened to the not exactly pretty sight of the remains of an airman who has been killed in a crash.

October 15, 1940

Effective October 1, 1940, I am promoted to the rank of Flight Cadet (*Fähnrich*).

October 17, 1940

Werneuchen is only a few miles outside the city limits of Berlin, and I am in the habit of spending every week end in the great metropolis. I usually stay at a small hotel just off the Friedrichstrasse. It did not take me long to discover all the cabarets and bars near the Zoo, along the Kurfürstendamm and Friedrichstrasse, besides the museums and theaters and famous buildings of Unter den Linden and the Lustgarten. Every week end I come back to a city of inexhaustible fascination. Each time I enjoy plunging into the whirl of gaiety in the great capital, whose glitter is still untarnished by war.

My motto: "Live life and learn its lessons."

I never seem to have enough money since coming to Werneuchen.

November 8, 1940

Flight Orders: "Flight Cadets Harder, Hopp, and Knoke, Flight Sergeant Kuhl, Flight Engineer Corporal Hense, are to proceed via aircraft Junkers 160, letters CEKE, to Münster (Loddenheide Airfield), for the purpose of taking over on transfer and ferrying to Werneuchen three aircraft, type Messerschmitt 109."

CEKE is a transport aircraft, late of the Lufthansa Airlines. Bad weather delays our take-off until 1000 hours.

Once in the air, we find it impossible to get the left wheel retracted, as the axle is broken. Kuhl is at the controls. We stay down low, at an altitude between 100 and 200 feet. The Flight Engineer tries to carry out repairs in mid-air, and after about 20 minutes he succeeds in doing so. We then climb up to an altitude of 500 or 600 feet. Kuhl hands over the controls to me and goes back to join Hopp and Harder, relaxing in the comfort of the cabin.

I detour to the south of Berlin and follow the main motor highway (*Autobahn*) to the west. Out of the haze on my left loom the radio masts of the transmitter at Königswusterhausen. Altitude 1,000 feet.

Something is wrong with the engine; fuel pressure drops sharply; I no longer seem able to maintain altitude. The engine gives a cough, sputters once, and then dies altogether.

"Hold tight—emergency landing!" I call back into the cabin. The Engineer beside me throws up his arms in front of his face. There is a dense forest below, and the radio masts to the left; but to the right is a nursery plantation about the size of a postage stamp. It is our only chance.

Too late, I notice the cables of a power line ahead. This is the end. Kuhl is beside me, his face white as a sheet.

I yank back the stick, and by a miracle the plane clears the power line by a matter of inches. The slipstream makes a whistling sound as the nose drops again.

And then the c—r—ash!

Great tree trunks snap like matchsticks, the left wing drops off, the fuselage slams on to the ground with a thud, slithering for another 100 feet or more, sweeping aside or crushing everything in its path.

Kuhl shoots forward head first into the instrument board.

There is silence—a deathly silence, broken only by the sound of 200 gallons of fuel pouring out of the shattered tanks.

Kuhl lies bleeding and unconscious. The Engineer seems to have been knocked out also. I am cut about the head. I try to push open the roof, but it is jammed. So is the door to the cabin. The smell of fuel drives me crazy. We are caught in a death trap, where we shall be cooked to a crisp if anything should catch fire. Frantic, I beat against the plexiglass windows with my bare hands.

Then I see the faces of Hopp and Harder outside, looking down at me from above. They kick at one of the panes until it breaks. We drag out Kuhl and the Engineer between us and lay them on the soft forest earth. They are alive. I try to administer first aid. Hopp and Harder go off to find help.

My head injuries are not serious.

Once again I have to return by train.

December 18, 1940

Three thousand future officers from the Army, Navy, Air Force, and SS elite guard *(Waffen-SS)* are assembled in the Berlin Sportpalast to await the arrival of the Führer and Supreme Commander of the Armed Forces. Three thousand keen young soldiers are nearly at the end of their period of training, and in a few months will go as officers to front-line operations. I am one of them.

Hitler is about to speak to us.

Of the Commanders-in-Chief of the three services, the first to arrive is Reich Marshal Göring. He and his staff find their seats on the vast stage. One of the Air Force Flight Cadets is personally presented to him, a tall, slim boy, whose face is pale and sensitive. His name is Hans Joachim Marseille, and he is already wearing the Iron Cross First Class. He won great distinction during the Battle of Britain as the youngest fighter pilot in the German Air Force. *(In another two years he is to be awarded the highest of all German decorations for valor, becoming the best-known fighter pilot in the Africa Corps and the one the enemy most feared.)*

Some minutes pass. Then, at an order, we spring up smartly to attention. "Here comes the Führer!" Right arms are extended in silent salute. There he is, walking slowly down the long center aisle to the stage, accompanied by Field Marshal Keitel and Grand Admiral Räder. Absolute silence reigns in that vast hall for several minutes. It is a solemn moment. Then Hitler begins to speak.

I do not suppose that the world has ever known a more brilliant orator than this man. His magnetic personality is irresistible. One can sense the emanations of tremendous will power and driving energy.

We are 3,000 young idealists. We listen to the spellbinding words and accept them with all our hearts. We have never before experienced such a deep sense of patriotic devotion toward our German fatherland. Here and now every one of us pledges his life in solemn dedication in the battles which lie ahead. *(Time and again in subsequent years our willingness to make the supreme sacrifice was tested. Most of the 3,000 were later killed in action on land, at sea, or in the air.)*

It is a deeply moving experience. I shall never forget the expressions of rapture which I saw on the faces around me today.

December 19, 1940

Today brought my posting orders, to No. 52 Fighter Wing (JG 52). I am to report to the Reserve Squadron of the Wing at Krefeld on January 2, and until then I can go on leave.

3

January 2, 1941

"Flight Cadet Knoke reporting to No. 52 Fighter Wing, sir, on posting effective January 2, 1941, from No. 1 Fighter School."

I am assigned to No. 1 Flight. Senior Lieutenant Öhlschläger, my Flight Commander *(Staffelkapitän)*, greets me without enthusiasm. He has a limp, effeminate sort of handshake. His face is bloated, with protruding eyes like a frog. I take an immediate and instinctive dislike to the man.

A little Lieutenant, looking like a schoolboy, comes into the room. I introduce myself, and I do not like him any better. He is very conceited. I do not know why: he does not wear any decorations. He looks the sort who would wet his pants at the first sign of battle.

The Squadron here to which I am posted is a reserve pool for the Wing. It consists of two Flights and a Headquarters Company. New pilots arrive here on posting from flying training schools at home, to receive a final polish before going on operations. They leave on posting to combat units as and when replacements are required.

There are several more Flight Cadets. We shall probably not be posted to operational units until after we have received commissions as Lieutenants. Meanwhile, our officers' training is to continue. All this never-ending business of going to school gets me down. To hell with it—I want to fly on operations! Nothing at all about the setup here appeals to me.

February 10, 1941

This Squadron has been transferred to the South of France. Of all places, we find ourselves in Cognac. We are based at a former French Air Force station. Fixtures and installations, we find, are very primitive, and the runways are badly constructed.

The old town of Cognac is gray and depressing. It is world renowned, however. The name speaks for itself and provides us with consolation for everything else, wherever there are bottles of the local product obtainable.

March 1, 1941

I have been promoted to the rank of Senior Flight Cadet (*Oberfähnrich*). I would have been happier with a posting to an operational unit.

Ever since the conclusion of the French campaign the air has become the focal point in the war. Our statistics make it plain that great success has been achieved by the German Air Force in its operations over the Channel and over England itself. A trial of strength of vital importance has been in progress for the last few months between the opposing forces engaged in air combat.

The fact still remains that victory in the Battle of Britain must be conceded to the fighter pilots of the Royal Air Force. As our opponent in the air, the Englishman we discovered to be tough, but a clean fighter. The story of the achievements of the British fighter pilots will always remain a glorious chapter in the history of air warfare.

Again and again the German High Command believed that the last of the doggedly fighting Spitfires must have been shot down. Yet again and again, as the days became weeks and the weeks became months, our bombers and fighters were still being engaged in combat by more fighters taking to the air, undaunted by the large numbers of the R.A.F. who crashed to their deaths every day.

If we failed to establish the air supremacy necessary for an invasion, that must be attributed entirely to the determination and courage of the British fighter pilots. In the final analysis it was they who made the German attack on the British Isles impossible.

The Supermarine Spitfire, because of its maneuverability and technical performance, has given the German formations plenty of trouble. "*Achtung*—Spitfire!" German pilots have learned to pay particular attention when they hear this warning shout in their earphones. We consider shooting down a Spitfire to be an outstanding achievement, as it certainly is.

I shall be curious to see what happens when I encounter my first Spitfire. For the present all is pretty quiet, even over the Channel.

The Battle of Britain seems to be over—and it is lost.

March 7, 1941

Back again in Germany.

The Squadron is stationed at Döberitz, just outside Berlin, and we form part of the air defenses of the capital. The Tommies come over only at night, however.

March 8, 1941

Another week end spent in Berlin. Yesterday I saw a girl friend from the old Werneuchen days. We spent some very happy hours together.

I never intended it, but I cannot help it: I seem to have fallen in love with Lilo. The Tommies are to blame for that. I was caught out in the streets during a raid on Berlin and had to go into a shelter. It was crowded with people, and I gave half my seat to a strikingly attractive girl. She was very reserved, however, and had hardly begun to thaw by the time the "All clear" sounded and we were permitted to leave the shelter. It was a long time before she would allow me to see her again.

And now I have to fall in love with her!

March 24, 1941

Lilo and I became engaged today. I think that we shall be able to get married in the autumn, subject to permission from the Personnel Branch. It is my birthday, too. I am 20 years old now. Still too young to get married, in the opinion of Senior Lieutenant Öhlschläger.

"Better wait until the war is over," he advises. But the war may drag on for 30 years, and I probably would not have the nerve to get married then. In any case, I do not want to wait so long before learning all about love.

Öhlschläger tells me to wait, but I can see what he has in mind. He keeps hovering round Lilo like a moth at a flame, and is liable to come to a sudden end if he persists in forcing his attentions on her.

April 25, 1941

IN THE NAME OF THE FÜHRER
I appoint
Senior Flight Cadet
HEINZ KNOKE
to the rank of
LIEUTENANT
effective April 1, 1941

I confirm this appointment in full expectation that through conscientious performance of his duty as an officer in accordance with his oath of service and loyalty, confidence shown by the award of this Commission to the above-named will be justified. He on his part may call upon the special protection of the Führer.

Dated at Berlin, this 22nd day of April, 1941.
(signed) GÖRING.
Reich Minister for Aviation and
Commander-in-Chief of the Air Force.

This document was handed to me today by the Commanding Officer, together with the ceremonial dagger of an officer.

Thus one ambition is now achieved. If only I could have an operational posting. . . .

May 22, 1941

"So long, Lilo! *Auf Wiedersehen,* my love!"

It is the station platform of the Schlesicher Bahnhof in Berlin, as the express begins to pull out. The train is crowded, but Lilo has somehow got to a window. We keep on waving until the train is out of sight. She is going to stay with my parents.

The military train for Cherbourg is at the next platform

and is due to leave a few minutes later. It is my train: the posting orders to front-line operations are in my pocket.

We roll out through the night, to the sound of the sirens. Tommy is over Berlin again.

May 23, 1941

No. 52 Fighter Wing has its Second Squadron based at Ostend. I find the headquarters located on the east side of the airfield, and report to the Commanding Officer, Captain Woitke. He is a huge man, and the force of his grip almost brings me to my knees when we shake hands. This is a welcome change after Öhlschläger and his flabby paw.

Woitke asks me several questions over a brandy in his quarters in the low station hut. I like this giant. He is a regular old regimental officer and an experienced pilot, with the Iron Cross First Class on his well-worn tunic. In the Battle of Britain he was credited with having shot down 15 British aircraft, mostly Spitfires.

At the end of half an hour he takes me over in his car to No. 6 Flight, to which I am assigned.

I am the fourth officer in the Flight. My Flight Commander is Senior Lieutenant Rech. Like the Commanding Officer, Lieutenants Barkhorn and Rall have the Iron Cross. Lieutenant Krupinsky has been here for only a week; but we have been together in the Reserve Squadron since January. The rest of the pilots are all experienced NCOs. They are good lads and know their job. They watch me rather suspiciously out of the corners of their eyes, and seem to have a low opinion of young Lieutenants. On learning that I am not a card player, they ignore me completely. At times like this, the proudly gleaming new rank badges are not worth a penny.

Outside, the Chief Maintenance Engineer shows me a camouflaged bay with my aircraft, a Messerschmitt ME 109E. He is grinning.

"An ancient crate; but it still manages to fly," is his verdict. "Still good enough for salvage" is what he really thinks.

An hour later I am up trying a few practice circuits. My landings are horrible. I am conscious by now that even the humblest privates are watching me incredulously. I do not seem to inspire much confidence here and it is all very embarrassing.

In the evening I am taken up again for operations practice with the Flight Commander. He seems to be satisfied.

May 24, 1941

Stand-to is at 0400 hours. The Chief drives us out to the field in his car. My aircraft is being armed. I have the engine run for a final check.

"All pilots to report to the Flight Commander!"

Senior Lieutenant Rech announces the operation orders for the day. The Flight is to carry out two patrol missions over the south coast of England. The first to take off at 0800 hours, the second at 1700 hours. The rest of the time we are at "five-minute readiness" in case of an alert. No. 4 Flight keeps a Section of four aircraft standing by ready for instant take-off.

This being my first mission, I am assigned to No. 3 Section, led by Lieutenant Barkhorn. I am to fly in tactical position No. 4, as wingman to Warrant Officer Grünert.

After briefing is over, everyone goes to sleep in armchairs and sofas until breakfast. I go outside, much too excited to sleep, and pace up and down among the aircraft until I become bored. Back in the crew room I try to read. After

I have been on ten missions I may be able to sleep too, like the rest of the boys.

At 0700 hours an orderly appears carrying two baskets. Breakfast! I find that I am hungry.

Senior Lieutenant Rech gets into his life jacket at 0750 hours.

"All right, fellows, let's go! Outside, everyone!"

The aircraft are wheeled out in front of the bays. My crate is at the far end of the dispersal area, next to Warrant Officer Grünert's. The latter strolls over and yawns.

"Remember to stick right by me, sir, if we should happen to land up in a scrap, no matter what happens. Otherwise you may find a Spitfire drilling a hole in your pants."

0755 hours. I have put on parachute harness. Mechanics give me a hand adjusting the straps.

0758 hours. I find the excitement terrific. The Chief has raised his hand. Canopies slam closed. Contact! The engine roars into life. We taxi across the field. In a few minutes the Flight is airborne.

Rech turns out to sea immediately. Visibility is poor, with cloud ceiling down to 500 feet. Behind us the land is out of sight in a matter of seconds. The horizon is barely discernible. More throttle, for my lumbering old crate is being left behind by the others, and I must keep up with them.

We head west, keeping down low over the water. The surface is calm. There are no signs of any ships or aircraft. Radio silence is maintained: the only sound is the monotonous drone of the engine.

A gray streak looms ahead: the English coast. We cross it north of Deal.

Rech flies inland for several minutes, following the railway tracks toward Canterbury. There is no traffic. People glance up at us, no doubt taking us for Spitfires in the haze.

Suddenly we encounter flak, coming up at us from the left. The tracers come up in orange-colored chains and look like pearl necklaces as they vanish into the clouds beyond us.

The Chief whips his aircraft round and dives after some target: I cannot make out what it is. My wingman also dives toward the ground, firing. I see it is a flak emplacement, sandbags round a 20-mm. pompom gun. Tracers flash right ahead, coming up at me. I set down the nose and fly low across an open field. Grünert makes a second attack. I adjust my sights and check over the guns. More and more pearl necklaces appear, in stark contrast against the dull gray overcast.

I never get to the point of firing. It is all I can do not to lose sight of Grünert. At any moment Spitfires may come swooping upon us out of the haze.

The Flight resumes formation and heads east, leaving behind something burning. I have not fired a single round. It makes me feel really foolish. True, I was much too excited to have hit anything: I must learn to keep much more calm.

There are fighter stations to the north of us, at Ramsgate and Margate. This time no Spitfires or Hurricanes appear. But suppose they were to come? I am at the rear of the Flight formation, and it is always the end man who is caught. More especially is this true of novices, and if they are also as excitable as I am . . .

0914 hours. Land at Ostend. I report to the Flight Commander.

"Well, how did you make out?" he asks. "Hit anything?"
"No, sir."
"Oh? Why not?"
"I never fired."

Rech laughs and pats my back: "Never mind: better luck next time. Rome was not built in a day, you know."

At 1705 we take off for the second mission.

This time none of us gets an opportunity to fire. We spend some time circling over the sea between Folkestone and Dover. The Tommy does not fly in such dirty weather; and it is even worse over the British Isles.

May 27, 1941

The Channel has been blanketed by heavy fog for the past two days. There was no activity on either side.

Today we were able to carry out a low-level attack on the Tommy airfield near Ramsgate. The weather kept us down to treetop height.

We took off on the first raid at 0715 hours. Grünert and I chose for our target the fuel dumps on the fighter station. No aircraft are visible. We strike at the airfield again and again, firing at every moving object. They put up some light flak; but their defenses are weak. A number of the fuel drums are on fire by the time we finish.

We return for a second raid at 1000 hours. This time I spot a flak emplacement at the west end of the runway. I come in to attack it from a height of only ten feet above the ground. But the Tommies stand firm and open up at me. Their fire passes close to my head: my fire lands in their protecting sandbags. I come in for two more runs at the target. Grünert is busy firing at a camouflaged bay, in which I can make out a Hurricane. My third attack is successful, and I see my 20-mm. shells bursting on the gun. The number-one gunner pitches out of the seat.

Suddenly the radio shouts: "Spitfires!"

Six or eight of them come closing in on us from the north. Not knowing exactly what to do, I keep close behind Grünert. There is a general mix-up which lasts for several minutes.

My comrades warn each other by radio when the Tommies attack. Grünert reminds me to stay by him.

We are at an altitude of only a few feet. My left wing tip almost scrapes the treetops when I whip my aircraft round after Grünert. A Spitfire just overhead flashes past. There is another one, staying for a few seconds in my sights, and I open fire. It immediately takes cover in the low overcast.

"Got it!" shouts somebody: I think it is Barkhorn. A Spitfire goes down to crash on the other side of an embankment.

The bastards can make such infernally tight turns; there seems to be no way of nailing them. Grünert spends several minutes trying to catch two of the Tommies flying close together; but they always break away and vanish into the overcast.

Fuel is running low: it is time to go home. I expect to see the red warning light at any moment. It is the same with the others.

Rech heads east.

When we land at Ostend, Sergeant Obauer is missing.

May 28, 1941

Tommy paid us a return visit. Blenheims and Spitfires have been coming over all day long.

It started in the early dawn at 0400 hours, as we were driving out to the airfield. A number of Hurricanes came sweeping in over the dikes and strafed our maintenance hangar.

The others took off to intercept. Unfortunately my aircraft is unserviceable until the afternoon. There is a leak in the pressure line to the undercarriage, and I cannot get the right wheel retracted.

At 1830 hours I finally take off with Barkhorn, Krupinsky, and Grünert. Blenheims accompanied by Spitfires are reported near Dunkirk. Our flak has already opened up on them—without any effect, of course. The flak people are always so proud of themselves whenever they get a chance to blaze away. They do not like being told by us fighter pilots that they never hit anything.

We climb to 20,000 feet. There is not a cloud in sight. We are dazzled by the sun setting in the western sky. I notice what I think may be enemy aircraft, until I realize that they are only tiny drops of oil on my windshield.

Base directs us to proceed to Calais: Blenheims have been reported in the vicinity. I am tense and eager as I scan the skies.

Suddenly Barkhorn whips round, heading back the way we have come. The Hurricanes are on our tails: it is the one place I never thought to look. They try to attack. We pull up in a long, almost vertical climb, then we swing sharply to the left, which brings us back on to their tails. They make off for the open sea; but our speed is greater. Inside of two minutes they are in range.

Then the dogfight is on. There is wild confusion, in which we all mill around in a mad whirl. I find myself on the tail of a Tommy and try to stay there. He has me spotted and pulls round to the left into the sun. I climb after him with every gun blazing, but I am dazzled by the sun. Blast! I try using my hand to shield my eyes, but it is no good. He has got away. I am so angry I could kick myself.

Grünert still shouts encouragement. I reply that I am no longer able to see. I have to give it up. And to think that this might have been my first kill!

In future I must take care to wear sunglasses.

May 30, 1941

"Patrol Area Dover-Ashford-Canterbury." So run our operation orders. "The milk run" is what old-timers in the Flight çall it.

The weather is cloudy: visibility poor. We are up for an hour and a half and land again without a sight of the enemy.

June 21, 1941

Three weeks have passed since the Squadron was last on operations.

We are now based at Suwalki, a former Polish Air Force station near the Russian border. Stukas and fighter-bombers use the field also.

For the past two weeks our armies have been massing in increasing strength all along the eastern frontier. No one knows what is happening. One rumor has it that the Russians will permit us to cross the Caucasus in a thrust to occupy the oil fields of the Middle East and the Dardanelles and seize the Suez Canal.

We shall see.

In the evening orders come through that the airliner on the scheduled Berlin-Moscow run is to be shot down. The Commanding Officer takes off with his Headquarters Section; but they fail to intercept the Douglas.

We spend the night sitting in the mess. The guesswork continues.

What is the significance of "Operation Barbarossa"? That is the code name for all the vast military activity in the east of the Reich. The order for shooting down the Russian Douglas airliner has convinced me that there is to be war against bolshevism.

June 22, 1941

0400 hours. General alert for all Squadrons. Every unit on the airfield is buzzing with life. All night long I hear the distant rumble of tanks and vehicles. We are only a few miles from the border.

0430 hours. All crews report to the Squadron operations room for briefing. The Commanding Officer, Captain Woitke, reads out the special order for the day to all the armed forces from the Führer.

Germany is to attack the Soviet Union!

0500 hours. The Squadron takes off and goes into action.

In our Flight four aircraft, including mine, have been equipped with bomb-release mechanism, and I have done considerable bombing practice in recent weeks. Now there is a rack slung along the belly of my good "Emil," carrying 100 five-pound fragmentation bombs. It will be a pleasure for me to drop them on Ivan's dirty feet.

Flying low over the broad plains, we notice endless German columns rolling eastward. The bomber formations overhead and the dreaded Stuka dive-bombers alongside us are all heading in the same direction. We are to carry out a low-level attack on one of the Russian headquarters, situated in the woods to the west of Druskininkai.

On Russian territory, by contrast, everything appears to be asleep. We locate the headquarters and fly low over the wooden buildings, but there is not a Russian soldier in sight. Swooping at one of the huts, I press the bomb-release button on the control stick. I distinctly feel the aircraft lift as it gets rid of the load.

The others drop theirs at the same time. Great masses of dirt fountain up into the air, and for a time we are unable to see because of all the smoke and dust.

One of the huts is fiercely blazing. Vehicles have been stripped of their camouflage and overturned by the blast. The Ivans at last come to life. The scene below is like an overturned ant heap, as they scurry about in confusion. Men in their underwear flee for cover in the woods. Light flak guns appear visible. I set my sights on one of them, and open up with machine guns and both cannon. An Ivan at the gun falls to the ground, still in underwear.

And now for the next one!

Round again, and I let them have it. The Russians stand fast and begin firing back at me. "Just wait till I take the fun out of your shooting, you bastards!"

Round yet again for another attack.

I never shot as well as this before. I come down to six feet, almost brushing the treetops in the process. Then pull up sharply in a climbing turn. My Ivans lie flat on the ground beside their gun. One of them leaps to his feet and dashes into the trees.

I carry out five or six more attacks. We buzz round the camp like a swarm of hornets. Nearly all the huts are in flames. I fire at a truck. It also burns after the first burst of fire.

0556 hours. Flight landing in formation.

The Chief sees smiling faces all round when the pilots report.

Aircraft are refueled and rearmed at top speed. The field is in a state of feverish activity. The Stukas return from their mission, in support of our armored units advancing on the ground. Their crews are jubilant, too.

0630 hours. Only 40 minutes after landing we are off again. Our objective is the same headquarters as before, and from a great distance we are guided to our destination by the smoke rising from the burning buildings.

This time considerable quantities of light flak come up to welcome us. It is just like that time near Canterbury. Once again I give special attention to the Ivans at their flak guns. This time I put down my bombs on one of the emplacements. Dirt and dust, the gun-site bursts! And that takes care of the Ivans.

The Russians appear to have taken cover and hidden their vehicles in the forest round the camp. We work over the forest systematically with our machine guns. Fires break out in different places. That must be where they have their fuel dumps. I fire at every target which presents itself to me, until the magazines are all empty.

We land at 0720 hours. Once again the Flight is prepared for action at lightning speed. Ground crews work with swift precision. We pilots help them and have to give them a full account of the operations. This time we set up a record by being completely ready in 22 minutes. We take off again immediately.

There is not much left of the Russian camp by now. Every target which we spot in the surrounding woodland is thoroughly strafed. I place my bombs on the last building which is still standing. Krupinsky does the same, which takes care of anything remaining. The camp is totally destroyed.

After 48 minutes in the air we land again and taxi over to the dispersal area. We now take a short breather and enjoy our first meal of the day.

New operation orders have arrived. Russian transport columns have been observed by our reconnaissance aircraft retreating eastward along the Grodno–Zytomia–Skidel–Szczuczyn highway, with our tanks in hot pursuit. We are to support them by bombing and strafing the Russians as they retreat.

Take-off at 1007 hours, accompanied by the Stukas. They

are to dive-bomb the Russian artillery emplacements in the same area.

We soon reach Grodno. The roads are clogged with Russian armies everywhere. The reason gradually dawns on us why the sudden surprise attack was ordered by our High Command. We begin to appreciate the full extent of the Russian preparations to attack us. We have just forestalled the Russian timetable for an all-out attack against Germany for the mastery of Europe.

This is one day I shall never forget. Our armies move forward everywhere, the spearhead units thrusting ahead. The Russians are taken completely by surprise. Soldiers on the roads on our side wave as we pass low overhead. The congested roads and lanes on the Russian side are subjected to concentrated bombing and machine-gun fire.

Thousand of Ivans are in full retreat, which becomes an utter rout when we open up on them, stumbling and bleeding as they flee from the highway in an attempt to take cover in the nearby woods. Vehicles lie burning by the roadside after we pass. Once I drop my bombs on a column of heavy artillery drawn by horses. I am thankful not to be down there myself.

We take off at 2000 hours for our sixth mission on this first day. There has been no sign of the Russian Air Force the entire day, and we are able to do our work without encountering opposition.

June 23, 1941

We take off on the first mission at 0445 hours. Again we set to work on the Ivan columns. It is a cold morning. Yesterday I was sweating all day long. When the sun is higher it will be unbearably hot.

Still no sight of any Russians in the air. Not until afternoon is any encounter with the Ratas reported. Then comrades from No. 4 Flight tell of an engagement with Russian fighters near Grodno. They note the primitive flying technique of the Ivans. Their aircraft are slow but surprisingly maneuverable.

Lieutenant Günther Gerhard, an old friend of mine from Fighter School days, is credited with a kill on his very first day on operations. He arrived from the Reserve Squadron only yesterday. Günther is an exceptionally fine pilot. I go over to the No. 4 Flight dispersal area after the last mission in the evening to visit him and congratulate him on bagging his "first." Captain Woitke shot down three Ratas in a single engagement.

June 25, 1941

The business of bombing is becoming increasingly distasteful to me. Comrades in No. 4 and 5 Flights have had two days of combat with Ratas. We who are engaged in bombing operations miss this fighting. It is high time for me to bag my "first."

The Army has been able to achieve success beyond the most optimistic expectations. The Russians are incapable of halting our advance. We are still endeavoring to overwhelm their retreating units. Their Air Force does not seem to be particularly eager for combat. Some of the Martin bombers attack targets in our rear, but without doing much damage. Russian fighter pilots evidently receive poor training. Their knowledge of combat tactics is as elementary as their aircraft are primitive. In a few weeks, however, they will have gained the necessary experience in combat. Despite amazing initial success, too much optimism would be a mistake on our part. The Russian soldier understands what he is fighting for: communism has turned every last one of them into a fanatic.

cumulus clouds drifting eastward across the sunny sky. The little engine putters away valiantly. Now and again I come down low over a field or a lake. Farmers are busy bringing in the harvest: swimmers are busy having fun in the water.

And I am soon to see Lilo again.

Three hours later I land at Prenzlau, refuel, and continue on the next leg of my flight to Lilo. Quite suddenly I run into bad weather. My good little Bücker is battered by rain squalls, and visibility becomes worse and worse. I am not going to reach Posen, which I had planned as my next stop. No sense in pushing on at any price. Lilo is not going to be interested in marrying an airman's corpse. I head for Werneuchen, landing there in pouring rain at 1631 hours.

August 27, 1941

I really want to start at 0600 hours, but am unable to obtain a clearance before 0830 hours. There is still a steady drizzle of rain, but visibility is better than it was yesterday. It takes nearly three hours' flying to reach Posen, where there is a flying training station.

Here again I have trouble with the control tower in getting clearance for Lodz. Damn the weather! All cross-country flights are canceled by order of the Met. Office. Damn it all! I wanted to be with Lilo tonight.

I stroll out to my aircraft. Flying instruction is confined to the immediate vicinity of the airfield. Seven or eight of the little training biplanes are taking off and landing all the time. Some Bücker Jungmanns are among them.

I have a brain wave. I start up my plane and taxi out to the runway. There is one of the pupils in the control truck busy entering in a logbook particulars of the flights.

He waves to me, then comes over to ask my name, since of course he fails to recognize me. I tell him that I am only going to do a few circuits and not to bother logging me. He then notices my rank badges, and clicks his heels, coming smartly to attention: "Very good, sir!"

I laugh to myself as I open the throttle. I make a couple of landings and wave to the boy in the control truck. Standing rigidly to attention, he raises his green flag, giving me a clear take-off.

This time I stay down low until I am behind some trees and out of sight of the airfield. I then set course for Lodz.

About 60 miles later I am in really heavy weather. The overcast ceiling drops to 100 feet. Visibility is reduced to danger point by blinding rain squalls. I am only a few feet above the ground, violently tossed and buffeted by the storm. There is astonishment on the upturned faces of people in the villages below.

Near Kalisch I strike the railway tracks on the line between Breslau and Lodz. The visibility ahead is practically zero. Whatever happens I must not lose sight of the line now. I shudder at the thought of a forced landing. A crash would be unavoidable, and a court-martial. Loss of a commission would make a fine wedding present for Lieutenant Knoke.

Suddenly the horizon becomes visible ahead. I am out of the rain, and the overcast ceiling is up at 3,000 feet.

A few minutes later I am over Schieratz. My father came here after the end of hostilities in Poland, and has been chief of police for more than a year. Lilo is down there, too.

I buzz the police headquarters. Lilo and my parents live in the building. I climb in an upward roll, and return for two or three more buzzes.

People come out and stand in the streets, craning their necks. A balcony door at my parents' apartment opens. My father, mother, and sister come out. And then Lilo, waving a large white towel. She is really there.

I do one more final run at the house, almost bouncing the wheels on the roof. Then I continue toward Lodz, where I land.

An hour and a half later Lilo is in my arms. When I tell her that we can be married tomorrow she cannot believe her ears. It is a surprise for my parents, too, since I had not let them know that I was coming.

August 28, 1941

All formalities prior to getting married are quickly completed in the morning.

At 1700 hours Lilo and I come out of the Registry Office as man and wife. Our apartment at home is like a flower shop.

I need say no more about this day. Our happiness is complete.

August 29, 1941

I am airborne again for several long hours. Stopping only to refuel at Frankfurt and Schwerin, I arrive back at the Flight at 1700 hours, and receive a rousing welcome from my comrades

There is an alert just before dusk, and I am off to intercept some Blenheims which have been reported near the coast. We do not succeed in finding them.

In the last couple of days I almost forgot about the war I am supposed to be fighting.

4

The North Sea coastline of Germany is now as familiar to me as the back of my own hand.

I have completed more than 100 missions, including convoy escort patrol work and alerts which occasionally result in an exchange of fire with Blenheims and Wellingtons in bad weather over the sea.

In the west the war has rather quietened down. Tommy seldom comes over now by day. After dark our night fighters have more work than we. The days have become quiet even over the Channel.

In the east our forces have won tremendous victories. German armored spearheads have reached the gates of Moscow. Now, however, winter faces the High Command with a number of serious problems which had not been anticipated. What the German soldier has to endure is monstrous beyond belief. The armies are not accustomed to the Russian winter, and their equipment is inadequate for such conditions. Urgent steps are being taken at home to remedy this situation as soon as possible.

Some of my old comrades in No. 52 Fighter Wing have been killed in action in recent months, but not before the score of enemy aircraft shot down to their credit had mounted.

I was informed that Günther Gerhard crashed on take-off and was fatally injured after he had shot down 18 Russians. Barkhorn and Rall are credited with having shot down more than 100 Russians. It is a keen disappointment for me not to have been able to stay with the old gang.

In the autumn the Flight was transferred for a few days to the Baltic area. We flew on practice maneuvers with the recently commissioned battleship *Tirpitz*. I had an opportunity of spending a few days as air-fighter control officer on board the great battlewagon.

We have been based at the new fighter station on the airfield at Jever since September. The Wing at present has Headquarters here also.

February 8, 1942

The North Sea islands are cut off from the mainland by ice. Apart from our regular operations, we run an emergency communications service there. Mail and food supplies are flown over, and civilians are transported in special cases of emergency.

February 10, 1942

The entire German Fighter Command in the west is on a general alert.

A part of the High Seas Fleet now at Brest, including the battleships *Prinz Eugen* and *Gneisenau* and several cruisers and destroyers, is to break through the Channel and proceed to Norway. It is anticipated that the British will do everything in their power to prevent our Navy from accomplishing its purpose.

The Channel is now the scene of as much activity as it was during the Battle of Britain. Constant vigil is maintained by our fighter units in the Channel area.

The Fleet is out.

The weather could not be worse. Flying is very uncertain, for the British as well as for ourselves.

In the evening we transfer to an airfield near the coast in Holland.

February 11, 1942

Fog keeps us grounded in the morning, but around 1000 hours the visibility improves. We sit around for hours ready to take off. We have to be able to be airborne within one minute.

Situation reports come in from the Channel. As we had anticipated, the British in fact are attacking, despite the very bad weather conditions. They send into action even their oldest types of aircraft. Our crews report combats with obsolete British torpedo-carriers of the Swordfish variety. Scarcely one of these aircraft is allowed to return to its home base. Heavy casualties are suffered by the British, but they continue fighting hard. It is another demonstration of courage by our old foe across the Channel.

Our airfield is swept by strong gales and frequent snow flurries, and we are obliged to remain grounded for the entire day.

February 12, 1942

The Fleet reaches the Straits of Dover and is reported in the vicinity of Calais.

The British still keep on flying their suicide missions. So far they have not once been successful in their attempts to strike at our Navy from the air. However, the long-range shore batteries in the Dover area have hit our ships, causing extensive damage.

The weather is on our side.

The Flight still remains grounded.

February 13, 1942

1016 hours. Alert for action!

It does not take long for the Flight to clear the snow-covered airfield.

Out to sea, the Fleet is under heavy attacks by the Tommies. They send into action the last of their remaining Swordfish. The British crews must know that they will never return.

We are to intercept a formation of attacking Blenheims. Visibility is still very poor. Our eyes try to penetrate the fog. The sea below is rough. Minesweepers come into view. The Flight Commander fires off the recognition flare signals. The ships are instructed to open fire on any approaching aircraft.

My aircraft is buffeted by sudden gusts of wind. It skims only a few feet above the white crests of the ominously surging green waves.

Calls from base constantly report the enemy positions. The farther we go out to sea, the worse the radio reception becomes. It is 15 minutes since we were airborne. According to reports from base, we may expect at any moment to encounter our Blenheims.

I adjust the reflector sights and set my guns ready to fire. Suddenly I observe some shadows, looming in the fog to our left.

There they are!

We all pull round at once. Everyone wants to get in the first shot. Sergeant Wolf, my wingman for the past six months, draws alongside. He nods his head, and I clearly see the white of his teeth through the plexiglass window as he grins broadly.

There are 12 Blenheims. There are 12 of us also. One for each. A Blenheim ahead is in my sights and I am ready to fire before he spots me. The Tommy pulls his aircraft up sharply, trying to dodge into the overcast.

I follow him round and keep my sights upon him. Fire! I press both buttons on my stick. I watch my tracers go into his left wing at a range of 150 feet, and then into the left side of the fuselage. We both bank steeply to the left. I keep my thumb pressing on the firing buttons. His left engine is hit. Wisps of cloud obscure my view. The bastard vanishes into the overcast.

Woomf!

The cockpit is full of flying splinters. Just over my right shoulder there is a large gaping hole. *Touché!* I also notice that two shell holes have appeared in my left wing.

There is the Blenheim again, just ahead. Once again I open fire. And then I am in the clouds.

The Tommy in front of me dissolves into a great shadow.

I now notice that my canopy has worked loose. I also smell burning. I gently throttle back and ease the stick forward. A few seconds later the sea is again visible.

What if my plane is on fire?

I cautiously turn round. The canopy mounting behind me on the right has been torn away, and the plexiglass window in the rear of the fuselage is missing.

By this time my Tommy is no longer in view.

Still the smell of burning persists. Damn it! What the hell can the matter be? My engine still runs smoothly: revs seem to be normal. According to the instruments there is nothing wrong. So what can be burning?

He hopes to be operational again within two days. His aircraft are being overhauled by maintenance crews, working day and night.

February 18, 1942

The officers' mess has some excellent French wine. Soon we no longer care how bad the weather is outside.

February 19, 1942

The third Flight is ready for operations once more. Eberle still has his troubles, however, as he is up for court-martial.

The meteorological service forecasts an improvement in the weather tomorrow. I must see that before I can believe it.

February 20, 1942

The aircraft are out in front of their bays and ready to fly. Driving snow is still sweeping across the field. The meteorological service continues to maintain the forecast of good weather. The pilots lounge around beside their planes, shivering and cursing.

At noon a bus transports them back to the quarters. The Met. experts still persist that the weather is improving. For once they turn out to be right. At 1535 hours the Squadron takes off.

It is to be hoped that the Tommies have not managed to send our big ships to the bottom of the sea in the meantime.

We cross the storm-swept Straits of Denmark (Skagerrak). After 50 minutes the rocky coast of Norway looms ahead. Skimming low over the wave crests, we enter Oslo Fjord.

Some 25 miles north of Oslo there is situated an isolated

landing strip up in the mountains. It is under deep snow, like the rest of the countryside below. Gardermoen.

Land at 1650 hours.

February 24, 1942

For three days we stay marooned up here in the mountains. The high peaks north of the airfield are hidden in the clouds. Three long days.

This morning a JU 88 equipped for blind flying takes off and sends us repeated radio reports of the weather along our course. They are favorable: we can fly.

Flying over the high mountain ranges of Norway is as hazardous as it is beautiful. The snow-clad peaks rise some 10,000 feet into the air, thrown into sharp relief by the deep valleys. West of us the mountains abruptly drop sheer into the sea. A number of German aircraft have been totally destroyed in recent months when compelled to come down on the jagged rocks and ice of the terrain below.

After nearly 90 minutes in the air, when fuel is down to the last drop, we land at Trondheim. I have never seen an airfield like this one. It is situated on a rocky plateau above the city and harbor. On the west and north sides the cliffs drop sheer into the Fjord, a deep gash in the landscape. The only runway is 2,500 feet long by 100 feet wide and is paved with wooden blocks. It has iced over after being swept clear of the loose snow.

February 25, 1942

A few feet above the runway the Commanding Officer and I set up the operations room in a little wooden hut. It is bitterly cold.

Last night the 36,000-ton *Prinz Eugen* slipped into the

Fjord. She has been seriously damaged by a mine and is to undergo extensive repairs here.

Our patrols maintain a constant air cover over the Fjord area. Their vapor trails stand out conspicuously against the icy air of the sky. It is anticipated that there may be attacks from the Tommies. They are not likely to let slip tamely through their fingers this fat prize which we guard.

According to the reports which I receive, nearly all our warships have suffered damage to a greater or lesser extent while running the Channel. The *Gneisenau* has put into port at Kiel.

February 26, 1942

At 1312 hours our sound detectors along the coast report the approach of a single enemy aircraft coming in at high speed. A reconnaissance?

At 1315 hours I take off from the field alone. I am determined to get the bastard. I climb to an altitude of 25,000 feet. Our patrol already in the air is ordered to continue circling above the *Prinz Eugen*.

Repeatedly I scan the skies for the intruder. There is not a Tommy to be seen. Reports from the ground are lacking in precision. They are of no value to me because they are too vague. After 85 minutes I give up and land again.

February 27, 1942

The intruder returns. I go up after him, but he eludes me again.

February 28, 1942

The Plotting Sergeant from the operations room next door comes bursting into my office, where I have been busy at my desk for some hours.

"Sir, that intruder is back again!"

I shoot out through the window and slither down the icy slope to the runway.

The alert is sounding. Already the ground crew is at work on my aircraft. Camouflaged screens are tossed into the snow and the canopy flaps open. Even as I fasten my safety belt the inertia starter begins to wail.

"Contact!"

The ground crews close the canopy and slide off the wing. I switch on the ignition, and the engine thunders into life. A cloud of glistening snow is whirled up high into the air behind me. I have to use almost full throttle to drag the plane through the deep snow.

A few seconds later I am airborne. Time: 1146 hours.

Base does excellent work today. I receive frequent position reports on the Tommy. Near Christiansand he crosses the coast, as he did yesterday and the day before. Altitude 25,000 feet.

Eighteen minutes after being airborne I have reached the same altitude as the intruder. "Bandit in Berta-Kurfürst—Hanni-eight-zero." So runs the message from base.

That means that the intruder is in map reference sector B-K, at an altitude of 25,000 feet. In that case I may spot him at any moment. The thin veils of ice cloud cause visibility to be somewhat reduced. I must keep a sharp lookout.

"Bandit now in Berta-Ludwig."

Damn! Where can the bastard have got to? I turn my head first to one side and then the other, looking in all directions. I run into a thin ice cloud and wheel off to the right.

Suddenly I tense inside. There he is, just a few feet overhead. A Spitfire. The R.A.F. rondel markings are the size of cartwheels.

With a jerk I lift the nose of my plane. I have to get him!

But by now he has spotted me also. He whips round in a tight turn toward me, drops his nose, and straightens out in a dive far below.

Throttle back: bank to the left. I must not lose sight of him. With both hands I pull the stick back hard into my belly while in a vertical bank; my body feels as if a giant hand is pressing it down into the seat, and for a moment my vision blacks out.

There he is again. He had put his plane into a vertical dive and is heading west for the open sea. I go down in a dive after him. At full throttle the noise of the engine becomes a frenzied scream, and the vibration causes the wings to quiver under the strain.

I adjust the sights and fire.

Must get closer range. To gain increased speed I close the radiator cooling flaps. Never mind if the radiator boils over; never mind if the engine goes to pieces; I have to get him, whatever happens.

The Spitfire zooms down like a meteor shooting through space. That plane is certainly a magnificent piece of work, and it is being flown by a lad who knows what he is doing and has plenty of nerve.

20,000 feet: he is in my sights, and I again open fire.

18,000 feet: range too great, estimate at 1,000 feet.

12,000 feet: my engine is beginning to boil.

10,000 feet: the dive is now even steeper than before.

6,000 feet: the Spitfire is faster. The distance between us increases. My eardrums are popping and my head feels like bursting. This vertical power dive is hell on a pilot. I have ripped the oxygen mask from my face. There is an overpowering smell of glycol. The engine has boiled. The oil temperature rises. Still the airspeed indicator registers over 500 miles per hour.

3,000 feet: slowly the Tommy straightens out from the dive. We both skim low across the snowfields in the high coastal mountains.

This Spitfire is a terrific plane. The gap between us widens steadily. We reach the open sea.

I give up the chase. My engine is about to seize. Throttle back; open the radiator flaps. My Tommy is now no more than a tiny speck on the horizon.

Coming round in a wide sweep until I am again heading for land, I fly up the sound to the Inner Fjord, hemmed in on all sides by the rocky precipices. Magnificent scenery, if one is in the mood to appreciate it.

Landing at 1303 hours.

I find that I am shivering. With rage as well as cold. Besides reaction after that power dive, which was certainly no picnic.

"Give me a double brandy!"

March 4, 1942

My Tommy has not put in an appearance for three days. The Commanding Officer has offered a bottle of genuine Hennessey brandy as a prize for shooting him down—a rare and valuable prize indeed here in the Far North.

Of course I am less interested in winning the Hennessey than I am in getting that bastard. I am a fighter pilot, and for that reason I have to get him.

March 5, 1942

A shout from the operations room: "There he is again!"

Out through the window and into the snow in one bound, 20 or 30 long strides, and I am in my aircraft. Seconds later I start rolling to take off.

1202 hours. Climbing steeply into the cloudless sky.

1210 hours. Altitude 15,000 feet. I adjust the oxygen mask. It is bitterly cold.

"Bandit in Cæsar-Ida—Hanni-seven-zero."

"Victor, victor; message understood," I reply.

Altitude 20,000 feet.

"Bandit now in Cæsar-Kurfürst."

"Victor, victor; message understood."

Altitude 22,000 feet: I shall climb to 25,000. I simply must get him today.

"Bandit in Berta-Ludwig."

He seems to be sweeping round the northern tip of the sound, heading up toward the anchorage of our warships.

I am now at 25,000 feet, scanning the skies around and below. Ahead and to the left I discern a tiny dark speck in the sky against the unbroken white landscape below.

It is the Spitfire, leaving a short vapor trail behind. The Tommy comes around in a wide sweep, heading up the Inner Fjord. I maintain altitude and study my prey. Now over his objective, the Tommy flies round in two complete circles. He is taking photographs.

I make use of this opportunity to take up a position above him. Apparently he is so intent on his task that he does not notice me. I am now about 3,000 feet above him.

Then he starts back on a westerly course. I open my throttle wide and check my guns as I swoop down upon him. In a few seconds I am right on his tail. Fire!

My tracers vanish into his fuselage. And now he begins to twist and turn like a mad thing. Must not let him escape. Keep firing with everything I have.

He goes into a dive, then straightens out again. He begins trailing smoke, which gradually becomes denser. I fire again.

Then something suddenly splashes into my windshield.

Oil. My engine? I have no visibility ahead, and am unable any longer to see the Spitfire. Damn!

My engine is still running smoothly. Apparently the oil in front of my eyes must have come from the badly damaged Spitfire when its oil-cooler was shot to pieces.

I veer a little to the right, in order to be able to observe the Tommy farther through the side window. He is gradually losing speed, but is still flying. The smoke-trail is becoming thinner.

Then another Messerschmitt comes into view climbing up on my left. It is Lieutenant Dieter Gerhard, my old comrade, and I radio him to say that I am no longer able to fire.

"Then let me finish him, Heinz!"

He opens fire. The right wing of the Spitfire shears away. Like a dead autumn leaf, the plane flutters earthward.

And the pilot? Is he still alive? My throat tightens. I had come to like that boy. If he is not dead, why does he not bail out?

The Spitfire goes down, a flaming torch now, hurtling toward the snowfield. It will crash there and be utterly destroyed. And with it the pilot.

I find myself shouting, as if he could hear me: "Bail out, lad, bail out!" After all, he is human, too; a soldier, too; and a pilot with the same love of the sky and clouds that I feel. Does he also have a wife, a girl like Lilo, perhaps?

"Bail out, lad, bail out!"

Then a body becomes detached from the flames and falls clear. A white parachute spreads open and drifts slowly down into the mountains.

A feeling of pure joy is in my heart now. This is my first combat victory in the air. I have got my man, and he is alive.

Dieter and I share the bottle of brandy. We drink a toast to our own fighter pilots, and another one to our Tommy.

Dieter brings him in, after landing in the mountains in a Fieseler Storch fitted with skis. He is a tall, slim Pilot Officer in the R.A.F. A stiff drink of brandy does him a lot of good. He joins in the laughter when I explain how the entire bottle was actually dedicated to him.

March 6, 1942

There is a surprise in the morning when orders arrive from Air Command Headquarters *(Luftflotte)* for our transfer back to Germany. The party last night in the mess did not stop at one bottle only, as my still-aching head reminds me.

At noon a Flight of fighter-bombers lands on the field. We hand over to them.

We commence the flight to the south in a cloudless sky. In the lead is a twin-engine Messerschmitt 110, fitted with an automatic pilot and direction-finding radio. We are to fly nonstop to Oslo *(Fornebu)*. The limited fuel capacity of our aircraft makes that the extreme limit of our range.

As always, I am once again fascinated by the beauty of the Norwegian mountain scenery, with its vast snow-covered expanses of glacier and icefield, broken by narrow ravines which are so deep that the sun cannot always penetrate to the bottom. Tiny little islands and rocks are dotted out to sea beyond the jagged coastal cliffs.

In an extended open formation we fly above, below, beside, and behind the leading Messerschmitt 110. My engine runs smoothly and so monotonously that it is almost an effort to keep awake. There is no talking over the radio.

We cross the high mountain ranges near Roros. The landscape is superb. Not so pleasant is the thought of having to make an emergency landing on this rugged terrain or descending by parachute into one of the precipices.

It seems that my fuel gauge is out of order. If the indicator is correct, I am burning up the stuff at three times the normal rate of consumption. Of course, that is not possible: I know from experience how economical my engine actually is.

I take a few photographs with my camera. They should make good pictures to send to Lilo. Lilo! She went a few weeks ago to stay with her aunt at Tübingen. We are going to have a baby shortly. In August she wrote. I begin calculating how long it was since we last saw each other. . . .

What is this?!! The red fuel warning lamp is on. Good God! but that is simply not possible. We have been airborne for only about 30 minutes.

There is a strong smell of gas. I become aware of it now for the first time. Could it be . . . ? Damn it all! If that is not just my luck, to run out of it here, where I can only go down somewhere into that icy waste!

I call Captain Losigkeit on the radio: "Jumbo-two to Jumbo-one; Jumbo-two to Jumbo-one: there is a leak in my gas tank or pipeline; no more fuel. Have five minutes for an emergency landing."

The Commanding Officer answers, cursing. There is nothing he can do to help, and we both know it.

"Jumbo-two leaving formation; closing down."

I have to go down to look for some landing place before the engine stops altogether.

"Good luck!" "Happy landing!" With good wishes the other comrades continue on their course. They cannot delay. Every minute is valuable for them also.

The mountains below are all more than 5,000 feet high. They are covered with broad snowfields, but examination on closer descent shows them full of crevasses and rocky boulders. Hopeless to attempt a landing there: the plane and I would be smashed to bits.

I am wide awake now, tense in every nerve. Ahead of me is a glacier, its tip leading into a tiny mountain lake. It is frozen and snow-covered. It is certain to be deep. Will the ice hold? It has simply got to be strong enough: there is no other choice.

I make preparations for the emergency landing. The touch-down must be very gentle, and exactly at the tip of the glacier. Throttle back; flaps down; propeller feathered. The ground rushes up quickly. The undercarriage remains unlowered. Easy now; contact is as soft as butter. Powder snow whirls high into the air. For 300 feet I skid across the creaking ice. Then my plane comes to a standstill. Throwing up the canopy, I jump on to the wing and haul my kitbag and a fur jacket out of the baggage compartment. The ice seems to be groaning under the weight. It is crackling and snapping. Will it break?

I run to the rocky shore and am thankful to feel terra firma under my feet again. It was a very near thing, and my knees are shaking. There have been many pilots who tried to make a forced landing up in this country, and it has cost their lives.

It is almost 1500 hours. In another hour they will be landing at Oslo and organizing my rescue. They have seen where I went down. However, today at least there is no chance of my being released from my predicament.

To the west of where I am I had noticed that there was a ravine running north and south. I walk for a few hundred yards through deep snow in a westerly direction. From the top of a rise in the ground I am able to survey the ravine. On the other side, and nearly 2,000 feet below, I notice a road. The sheer precipices are an insuperable barrier for me. Otherwise there is no sign of human life anywhere, as far as I can make out.

My aircraft is still resting flat on the ice. I think that it will prove strong enough to bear the weight. I shall have to spend the night in the cockpit.

I begin to feel hungry. In my knee pocket I have some chocolate and a few cigarettes. These will last me until morning. It is just as well that I thought of stowing my fur jacket into the baggage compartment before we left. It comes in useful now, for it is getting colder.

When darkness falls I unpack my parachute and drape the voluminous folds of silk around me. That keeps me warm. Then I worm my way into the seat and close the canopy. In the night I watch the driving snow clouds scudding across the sky, until I fall asleep in the seat.

March 7, 1942

Several times during the night I wake up, stiff and aching from the cramped position. Often I stretch my legs by taking a short run around in the snow. About midnight it starts snowing heavily. By morning only the tail and a propeller blade remain visible from my Messerschmitt.

Light snow is still falling. I cannot see for more than a couple of hundred feet ahead. Rescue by air is out of the question. Are they ever going to find me?

There is no sense in my attempting to set off on foot, for I would soon lose all sense of direction in the blizzard. It is 0800 hours. I eat a slab of chocolate and then chew a cigarette. I chew it because I have no light. It has the effect of deadening the hunger.

I remain in the aircraft, as it is warmer there, but now and again I stretch my legs outside. I fiddle about with the instruments and discover that the electrical equipment is still intact. I fire the guns a few times. Little fountains of snow spurt up where the bullets hit the lake shore. The noise echoes and re-echoes through the silence of the mountains. It must be audible miles away.

Hour after hour I patiently wait. Have they started the search for me by this time? I chew some more cigarettes. I am really hungry. The nicotine in the tobacco soothes the pangs.

The snow never stops. It is 1400 hours. There is a rising wind, and it is becoming uncomfortable.

Every hour I fire off a short burst with my guns. If the weather clears in the night I shall send up signal flares.

I lose all sense of time in the eternity of waiting. It is night again. The snow comes driving across the glacier lake as it is lashed by the gale.

The parachute silk is soft—soft like the dress on a beautiful woman. . . . It is easy enough for my thoughts to wander, but finding a way out is something else again. I am chilled to the marrow and spend hours just sitting there, shivering like a dog, in spite of the fur jacket and parachute silk. It is probably lack of food. My stomach revolts at all the tobacco I have chewed.

I try to sleep, feeling sick and cold and hungry.

March 8, 1942

It is noon again. The snow has stopped. They must find me today: I have to get out of here. I keep firing short bursts. They must find me today.

At 1600 hours I hear the sound of a dog barking. Next minute a beautiful Irish setter appears and gives me a vociferous welcome. Shortly afterward I am shaking hands with a Senior Lieutenant from an Alpine Regiment.

March 9, 1942

During the night they took me in to Oslo by car. I report at once to the Duty Officer at Air Command Headquarters (*Luftflottenkommando*).

I was able to have a good long sleep this morning in the hotel room which was placed at my disposal. At noon a transport aircraft leaves the airport bound for the Reich. It is to land me at Aalborg in Denmark. That is where the Losigkeit Squadron is now grounded by bad weather.

March 10, 1942

There was quite a reception when I rejoined my comrades yesterday. They all envy me my beautiful Irish setter, Turit. I had to buy him from the Alpine troops.

At 1511 hours we land back at Jever. Turit lay quietly in the baggage compartment behind the armor plate at my back while we were in the air.

The special duty Squadron is disbanded. Dieter and I return to our old Flight.

June 21, 1942

I have now completed more than 150 operational missions since returning from Norway, on patrols over the North Sea from the bases at Jever, Wangerooge, and Husum.

All the pilots are experienced airmen and grand types. The Chief is Captain Dolenga, I am his second in command, and Lieutenant Gerhard, whom I knew back in No. 52 Fighter Wing, is our Engineer Officer. Lieutenant Steiger joined the Flight a few months ago. This tall, fair-haired lad is a brilliant pilot who shot down his first Blenheim in an attack on one of our Navy convoys a few days ago.

Warrant Officers Maul, Voget, and Dobrik are old soldiers. All won the Iron Cross First Class during the Battle of Britain. Flight Sergeants Wenneckers and Raddatz started combat flying in Holland a year ago. Sergeant Biermann, a little man from Berlin, came to the Flight here from Russia, like me. At the beginning of the war he was with the Infantry in Poland.

Ground-crew personnel also consist of fully qualified technicians. For the most part they were skilled craftsmen in civilian life. Only a small fraction is formed by regular professional soldiers, like the pilots.

For nearly a year Corporal Arndt has been my crew chief. This faithful lad, our Messerschmitt 109, and I together form an inseparable trio (*and remain so for years to come*).

It would not be right if we forgot our long-legged friends. Turit, my setter, is beautiful and spoiled and as temperamental as a prima donna; for he is the fastest dog in the Air Force. Fips, our monkey mascot, is an anarchist at heart: he has no idea of discipline. At an inspection parade he once stole a cap belonging to a visiting Colonel and vanished with it on to the hangar roof. It was the most amusing parade I have ever attended. Fips has been warned to expect a posting to the Russian front as a result. Perhaps he will be our secret weapon; for once the Russians have seen him they will be laughing so much they will be incapable of shooting.

And so we all live together as airmen, in a strange little world of our own, at the end of the runway.

June 22, 1942

It was a surprise yesterday evening when a section was detached from the Flight and transferred to Holland under my command. For operational purposes I come directly under the Division Headquarters, where the most up-to-date method of fighter control and interception in the world is being put into effect.

Overnight our aircraft are equipped with the new ultra-short-wave radios. My orders are to carry out extensive tests of a technical nature under operational conditions of the new "Y" system, and for this purpose I am given a free hand and wide authority. Amongst other documents from Division Headquarters I receive the following written authorization:

> Lieutenant Knoke is attached to the Twelfth Air Corps Experimental Unit for special flying duties in connection with High Command (OKL), this work is to be considered essential for the prosecution of the war.
>
> Certified that he is hereby authorized to land at all airfields, including those outside the limits of the First Fighter Division and Twelfth Air Corps Areas.

The signature is that of a Major on the General Staff at Division Headquarters.

The introduction of the new "Y" system results in vastly improved long-distance radio communications between aircraft in flight and the ground. Operationally speaking, it will now be possible for our fighters to be located and directed by ground control at all times.

The control room itself is in an enormous bombproof concrete shelter. In the center stands a huge map of Holland on plate glass about 30 feet square. On the far side of this giant map there is a raised platform, with Air Force girls sitting at a battery of headphones and microphones. The girls receive reports of approaching enemy aircraft from radar stations along the coast, and project lights which are moved across the map to maintain a continuous plot of their positions. Other girls locate our own fighters by means of the "Y" system, and plot their positions on the map also.

In front of this map there is another raised platform, equipped with a complicated arrangement of microphones and switches. From here every single fighter formation can be directed by ground-control officers individually by ultra-short-wave radio telephone. A glance at the map is all that is required to obtain a complete picture of the changing situation at any given moment.

The entire scene is presided over by the Division Commander sitting at the control desk with his Senior General Staff Officer and Chief Intelligence Officer.

This is where all the radio, telephone, and teletype communications in the Division Area converge. There is an adjoining office, where weather reports are received from all the meteorological stations and plotted before they are passed to the main control desk. Two other floors in the building are taken up with offices of the headquarters of the operational, administrative, and technical services.

Approximately 1,000 officers, NCOs, soldiers, technicians, meteorologists, administrative officials, and a large number of very pretty girls keep this fighter-control headquarters functioning as a directing brain by day and night.

August 18, 1942

During the past two months I have completed more than 200 test flights. We were attacked by Spitfires on several occasions over the Schelde Estuary, and we were often far outnumbered. We had several narrow escapes.

The experiments with the "Y" system have produced most satisfactory results. Every Fighter Wing in the west is being equipped with the apparatus we have tested. Other fighter-control headquarters of a similar type are being constructed at Stade, Metz, Munich, Vienna, and Berlin.

The Air Force High Command are preparing in anticipation of intensified air attacks on Reich territory to come as a result of the Americans entering the war.

October 2, 1942

The ME 109E was replaced several months ago by the improved 109F. A few days ago the first models of the "G" type started coming off the assembly lines. The performance of the "Gustav" (as we call the ME 109G) seems, for the time being at least, to be definitely superior to that of the Spitfire.

Captain Marseille, whom I met at the Berlin Sportpalast as a Flight Cadet nearly two years ago, was credited with having shot down no fewer than 16 Spitfires during a single mission in his Gustav. A few weeks ago he received from the hands of the Führer personally the highest German decoration for valor, after he had brought down 150 of the enemy in the skies over Africa.

Two days ago, still undefeated by the enemy, Hans Joachim Marseille met death—an airman's death near El Alamein. The engine of his Gustav suddenly caught fire in mid-air. With a score of 158 combat victories to his credit, Marseille bailed out, but his parachute snagged on the tailplane. Comrades brought back his body from the desert. We have lost the No. 1 German fighter ace.

Something very queer happened today, just a few hours after we learned about the death of Marseille.

At 1215 hours we had an alert. I took off with Flight Sergeant Wenneckers as my wingman. A Mosquito was reported on reconnaissance in the Oldenburg area.

Wenneckers kept dropping farther and farther behind. At 12,000 feet I lost sight of him altogether.

I called him by radio but could get no answer. Then I

noticed the flaming wreckage of an aircraft which had just crashed on the broad plain far below.

Wenneckers . . . ?

The Mosquito was far away before I could reach its altitude. I gave up the chase and descended in three or four wide spirals to Jever.

I landed, and then I could hardly believe my eyes. Wenneckers himself was there, laughing at me. His Gustav had suddenly caught fire in mid-air for no apparent reason, in exactly the same way as the plane Marseille was flying in Africa three days ago. The fire started in front of the engine, which continued running smoothly.

We are baffled by the mystery. A few days ago No. 4 Flight also lost a Gustav in precisely similar circumstances. Reports coming in from other Squadrons are to the same effect.

I begin to look at my plane with some misgiving.

October 31, 1942

A few days ago Captain Dolenga was posted to night fighters. I am acting Flight Commander for the time being.

Despite bad weather we carry out convoy-escort patrols from early morning in conjunction with the Navy.

At 1414 hours a report comes in that Blenheims are attacking our convoy. Two minutes later I am airborne together with Lieutenant Gerhard. Our patrol over the sea is already engaged in combat. The Section leader, Flight Sergeant Dobrik, calls for assistance. Fuel is low, and they will be obliged to land in a few minutes.

I reach the convoy within ten minutes. Off to the north the comrades are engaged in a brisk dogfight with four Blenheims. One of them is in flames by this time, and a few seconds later crashes into the sea. The others attempt to escape in the haze. I do not lose sight of them and prepare to attack the tail-end Blenheim.

After giving it a prolonged burst of fire with all my guns, I notice that its right engine is on fire. It climbs steeply up into the low clouds, where nothing remains visible except a reddish glow.

After I have landed, a report is received from one of our crash boats of a Blenheim having been seen falling in flames out of the overcast and going down into the sea in map reference sector Anton-Quelle-three.

That aircraft must be mine, and so I am credited with my second kill.

November 6, 1942

1200 hours. From Division Headquarters comes a report of two Mosquitoes approaching. At the same moment there is a ring at my telephone. Lieutenant Kramer, our Fighter Control Officer at Division, calls to ask if I can fly in the bad weather.

I reply in the negative. Cloud ceiling is down to 100 feet, and visibility is impossible. I cannot even see across to the other side of the field.

"Sorry, Kramer, it cannot be done. Anyway, in this sort of muck the two Tommies will come down on their snouts without our help."

For several hours it has been raining—a steady, persistent drizzle. The pilots sit around, playing cards or writing letters home, or lie sleeping on camp cots in the next room.

I plot the progress of the Mosquitoes from the position reports as they come in. They actually fly inland over the heart of the Reich. Inside of an hour they are reported to be over Berlin, and our flak opens up on them. Those boys must have guts all right. Weather like this makes flying anything but a picnic.

The telephone rings again.

"No. 5 Flight; Lieutenant Knoke speaking."

The call this time is from Colonel Henschel, commanding fighter defenses in the North Sea coastal area.

"How is the weather at your end, Knoke?"

"Just as bad as it can be, sir. I can see only for a few yards."

"Knoke, you will have to fly, and that is all there is to it. I have just had a telephone call from Reich Marshal Göring. He is in one of his rages. Why are we not in the air? The weather is too bad for us to fly; yet those confounded Tommies can get over Berlin. Do you imagine I would tell that to the Reich Marshal? Those Mosquitoes are to be shot down at all costs. Do you understand?"

"Yes, sir."

"Which of the pilots are you going to send?"

"Flight Sergeant Wenneckers and myself, sir."

"Very well—and the best of luck to you!"

"Thank you, sir."

Wenneckers and I are the only pilots in the Wing with experience in blind flying. This is not the first time that we have set off together in dirty weather.

Take-off 1330 hours.

I can see hardly anything ahead. This blasted rain! Keeping down low, we hurtle over the rooftops, trees, and power lines. Radio reception from the ground is good. Lieutenant Kramer directs me.

The Tommies are heading northwest over the Bremen area. From past experience they may be expected to cross the East Friesian Islands.

I head for the coast. The weather over the sea is not any better.

The most recent report gives the position of the Mosquitoes as map reference sector Berta-Quelle-eight, on course three-one-five. At any moment now we may sight the bastards, if we keep our eyes peeled. If only it would stop raining! We have to concentrate our attention on not running into some obstruction.

Time: 1347 hours.

I am unable to see anything at all ahead. It is maddening. Base calls: "You should see them now. Try a little to the left."

I do not answer, for a shadow suddenly looms out of the grayness ahead. It is a Mosquito.

He has spotted me also and whips round to the left in a vertical bank, almost dipping his wing tip in the sea. Now he twists round to the right. Then he dodges to the left again.

"No, no, my friend, it is not such a simple matter to shake off Knoke." Every time he turns I fire in front of his nose.

We are flying low, very low, heading out over the open sea now. My Tommy leaves a faint trail of smoke. At full throttle he follows a steady course of three-two-zero. He moves at such a blasted high speed. But my good Gustav is just able to maintain the pace. I stay on his tail. Wenneckers gradually falls behind. The terrific speed is too high for his plane.

I want to fire at only the closest possible range, and hence try to close the gap between us. Slowly, almost imperceptibly, I draw nearer to my opponent. I shut the radiator flaps, and the range drops to 150 feet. He is squarely in my sights.

"Fire, Knoke, fire—NOW!!"

I press both firing buttons. The burst catches him in the

left engine. The plane is constructed of wood. The wing goes up in flames at once and shears off at the root. A few seconds later one De Havilland Mosquito vanishes into the green depths of the North Sea.

That was my third.

Nothing but a sludge of oil is left on the surface. I mop the sweat from my face.

December 23, 1942

At 1150 hours I return from a convoy-escort patrol over the sea. Ten large freighters, accompanied by a destroyer and four motor torpedo boats, are out in the Weser Estuary. At high tide they will put in to Bremerhaven.

At 1257 hours I am out there again. On the decks of the ships the crews stand waving as we pass overhead. They will be happy to be in port this evening.

After 20 minutes in the air I receive orders to land. Scarcely have I landed, and my aircraft has only just been refueled, when there is an alert.

Blenheims off the coast are heading for our ships. We intercept them off Norderney. There are two of the enemy aircraft, but the moment they notice us they vanish into the overcast and do not reappear. Too bad! This is my hundred and fiftieth operational mission. I would have liked to celebrate the occasion by adding one more to my score.

It is Christmas Eve tomorrow. Lilo is coming with Ingrid, our little daughter.

December 24, 1942

Christmas Eve.

No activity on either side. Friend and foe alike observe a tacit truce.

Lilo and I are together again. For the first time there are three of us under the glittering Christmas tree. I hold little Ingrid in my arms. Her tiny hands reach for the lights on the tree.

There is a strange, peaceful silence all around. Lilo kisses our child and me. Her lips are half open, in warmth and tenderness. The perfume of her dress blends with the aroma of pine needles. A spirit of joy and happiness pervades the room.

Dieter Gerhard quietly joins us. He kisses Lilo's hand and wishes us a merry Christmas. He and I later go over together to the quarters of the men in the Flight. There we make the rounds, visiting every room. The soldiers have decorated them all with Christmas trees or fir branches. Now they are lying around on their beds, reading, smoking, thinking, or sitting at tables, writing, or playing card games.

"Merry Christmas, everybody!"

"Thank you, sir, and the same to you!"

Dieter and I walk slowly back together later to my quarters. There is snow on the ground. This is unusual where we are, so close to the sea. The clear sound of an accordion being played comes over from the Headquarters Company billet: "*Stille Nacht, heilige Nacht. . . .* Silent night, holy night."

This is the most beautiful of all German carols. Even the British, the French, and the Americans are singing it tonight. Do they know that it is a German song? And do they fully appreciate its true significance? Why do people all over the world hate us Germans and yet still sing German songs, play music by such German composers as Beethoven and Bach, and recite the works of the great German poets? Why?

Far into the night Dieter and Lilo and I sit around together in my cozy living room, in comfortable deep armchairs beside a fragrant bowl of hot punch. In reminiscent

mood, we two men recall the events of the year now drawing
to its close. How many times we used to sit around this same
table together with Captain Dolenga and Lieutenant Steiger.
Gerd Steiger . . . that quiet, tall, fair-haired lad, shot down
before our eyes by a Mosquito over the south side of the
airfield. . . . We found his body under the half-open parachute. . . .

Lilo listens to us in silence. She smiles and strokes Dieter's
long, straight hair. He is not too steady on his feet when he
gets up to go. Our punch seems to have been rather too much
for him. I take him to his room.

When I return, Lilo is leaning thoughtfully against the
bedroom door, gazing in the the half-light at Ingrid on her
tiny cot. Our child is quiet and peacefully asleep.

At last we are alone, alone together. . . .

5

January 27, 1943

On January 7, I was placed in charge of the training course for new NCOs which is organized every winter by Second Fighter Division. I also had to run the course last year. Consequently I am known in the Wing as "the last of the Prussians." I have to put up with this nickname, even though I do not care for it. We airmen generally do not think much of the spit-and-polish variety of drill parades, although we accept any training which increases the fitness, toughness, and fighting efficiency of the soldier.

Toughness and fighting efficiency are coming to be of vital importance to every single German soldier. The war has imposed upon us unbelievable hardships. Russia has cost us the greatest effort and heaviest sacrifices. A few days ago we lost Stalingrad. The greatest battle in the history of this war has thus come to an end.

Addressing my NCO students, I watch their grim faces as I describe to them briefly the vast pincer operation which has resulted in the encirclement and annihilation of the German Sixth Army.

I go out to the runway alone. The regiment from my home town formed part of Paulus' Army. I know that the regiment

contained many of my classmates and a large number of
Hamelin boys, companions of my youth. They were enticed
away from their mothers by a new Pied Piper.

Looking out across the broad expanse of snow, I can vis-
ualize the graves—the thousands upon thousands of graves,
each marked with a steel helmet upon a wooden cross—
stretching to eternity through the Russian winter. . . .

At noon comes the first attack by American bombers on
the North Sea coast of Germany. We have been expecting it
for several weeks. The enemy consists of formations of heavy
four-engine Consolidated Liberators and Boeing B17s. The
Boeings are known, and with good reason, as "Flying Fortresses." And that is exactly what they are, with exceptionally heavy defensive armament which creates some very
severe problems for our Fighter Command.

Our Intelligence Service has kept us supplied for months
with a constant flow of information about these giant planes.
Bit by bit we are able to familiarize ourselves with every
technical detail of their performance. As fighter pilots we are
particularly interested in the defensive armament. Sixteen
super-heavy machine guns are so arranged that no blind spot
is left anywhere within range of the aircraft.

I have spent hours in lectures and discussions with the
other pilots, determining the best tactical moves. Models are
quickly constructed and used for demonstrations of approaches from every angle and in every position. Every
minute of our spare time is occupied in an infinite variety of
calculations of the various speed allowances for different
forms of attack. Long target tabulations are compiled,
sketches and plans are drawn, new models are hurriedly
constructed.

From the moment our Fighter Squadrons stationed in the
Channel area first make contact with the enemy and engage

in combat with the Flying Fortresses, reports are sent in continuously to our best fighter pilots for analysis and interpretation down to the last, minute detail.

During raids on targets in France the first of the Fortresses and Liberators are shot down. Thus the spell is broken: the myth that these monsters are invulnerable is ended.

Intensive briefing of air crews in the fighter and interceptor wings assigned to the defense of the Reich continues, in preparation for the fierce air battles that are anticipated.

Construction of an intricate network of radar screens and the establishment of additional ground control bases complete with "Y" stations and the most up-to-date two-way radio equipment have greatly facilitated aircraft interception and directed pursuit over wide areas.

It is obvious to me that today, with the first massed daylight attack by the Americans on Germany, marks the opening of a new phase of the war in the air.

During the evening I telephone to my Flight at Jever. Dieter Gerhard and Lieutenant Frey, who is acting as Flight Commander at the moment, have brought down their first heavy bombers. They are seething with excitement there. Sergeant Müller was shot down but succeeded in parachuting to safety.

I then telephone a request to the Division Commander for immediate posting back to my Flight. At a time like this I feel that my place is with my comrades.

I leave for Jever the same night.

February 4, 1943

From early morning we have been standing by ready to take off, in case of an alert. Our radio direction-finders report heavy concentrations of enemy aircraft over the Great Yarmouth area.

I am eager to go after them. Flight morale is in a superb state. There is no question but that every one of the comrades will put on his best performance when the show begins.

1113 hours. Take-off to intercept. One minute later I am airborne in formation over the field. The 11 aircraft in my Flight close up alongside.

Message from base: "Heavy babies in sector Dora-Nord-pol. Go to Hanni-eight-zero."

That means that the bombers are east of Leuwarden and I am to climb to 25,000 feet.

Then the gremlins go to work on my engine. At 15,000 feet it begins to sputter. My plane cannot climb any higher.

I call Dieter and he takes over command.

In an overpowering frenzy of rage I peel off and spiral down to land. The mechanics rip the cowling from the engine. What is the matter with my blasted crate?

Some obstruction in the pump prevents the engine from obtaining sufficient fuel at high altitudes. The mechanics work like mad to correct the trouble.

Thirteen minutes later I am back in the air.

"Heavy babies now in Friedrich-Paula."

That is far away off to the south. I open up the throttle. The engine is running well now. At 20,000 feet I pass through a cloud layer. I must catch up with the formation.

25,000 feet: "Heavy babies in Gustav-Paula."

The bastards are heading south, something like 150 miles away.

"Follow course two-zero."

Now, what does that mean? Why am I supposed to turn round and head in the opposite direction? In some hesitation I swing the plane round. My inquiry to base is answered with an order to land.

I am down at 1258 hours. Two minutes later the comrades appear over the field and land also.

Lieutenant Kramer, our Control Officer, telephones. He tells me that the Americans reached the southern tip of the Zuider Zee and then turned tail and headed for home. No bombs are reported dropped.

There is no time for me even to swear. At 1308 hours I have to take off again for another convoy-escort patrol. This is a monotonous duty which I have come by now to detest.

February 26, 1943

What a day!

I am feeling just in the mood for a good scrap with a swarm of Americans. The weather is ideal, the sky a clear and cloudless blue.

Over Great Yarmouth everything is quiet as yet.

The pilots lie around outside on the tarmac, wrapped up in blankets, enjoying the warmth of the first spring sunshine. I relax beside them, squinting idly up at the sky.

The two big loud-speakers blare out dance music. We enjoy the BBC musical programs for German soldiers. When the announcer starts his propaganda there is ironic laughter and applause.

"Shut your mouth, man, and get on with the music!"

Suddenly the music stops.

"Attention, all! Attention, all! Lieutenant Knoke is wanted on the telephone!"

Division is calling: fresh enemy concentrations are reported in map sector Dora-Dora. So the Yank is getting ready off Great Yarmouth for another raid again.

At 1050 hours we are ordered to stand by. The Yank is off the coast and heading for Wilhelmshaven.

1055 hours. Intercept!

Canopies close. Mechanics swing the starters. My engine at once thunders into life. I turn to watch the others starting.

All clear! The 12 aircraft take off together in formation.

I turn on the radio and call base:

"Elbe-one calling Bodo. Elbe-one calling Bodo. Report victor."

"Bodo calling Elbe-one. Bodo calling Elbe-one. Victor, victor."

Contact with the ground is good. We climb quickly up 25,000 feet.

"Heavy babies in Anton-Quelle-eight. Remain over the airfield."

I turn north. Our engines leave heavy vapor trails streaked across the clear blue of the sky. Then I spot the enemy formation ahead.

It is an impressive sight. Some 300 heavy bombers are grouped together, like a great bunch of grapes shimmering in the sky.

I check my guns and adjust the reflector sight.

The enemy mass is still several miles away and heading south. I report my observations to base. It will be just like a beehive down there now: I cannot help smiling at the thought of the turmoil.

We draw closer to the bomber formation. I must have opened the throttle unconsciously. I can distinguish the individual enemy aircraft now. Most of them are Liberators. They look as if their fat bellies were pregnant with bombs. I pick out one of them as my target.

"This is where I settle your hash, my friend," I mutter.

I shall make a frontal attack. The Yank is focused in my sights. He grows rapidly larger. I reach for the firing buttons on the stick. Tracers come whizzing past my head. They have opened up on me!

Fire! I press both buttons, but my aim is poor. I can see only a few hits register in the right wing.

I almost scrape the fat belly as I dive past. Then I am caught in the slipstream, buffeted about so violently that for a moment I wonder if my tailplane has been shot away. I climb up steeply and break away to the left. Tracers pursue me, unpleasantly close.

Damn all this metal in the air!

Three hundred heavy bombers carry a total armament of 4,800 super-heavy machine guns. Even if only one in ten has a chance to fire that still means we run into quite a barrage.

I come in for a second frontal attack, this time from a little below. I keep on firing until I have to swerve to avoid a collision. My salvos register this time.

I drop away below. As I swing round I turn my head. Flames are spreading along the bottom of the fuselage of my Liberator. It sheers away from the formation in a wide sweep to the right.

Twice more I come in to attack, this time diving from above the tail. I am met by heavy defensive fire. My plane shudders under the recoil from the two cannon and 13-mm. guns. I watch my cannon shellbursts rake along the top of the fuselage and right wing, and I hang on to the stick with both hands.

The fire spreads along the right wing. The inside engine stops. Suddenly the wing breaks off altogether. The body of the stricken monster plunges vertically, spinning into the depths. A long black trail of smoke marks its descent.

One of the crew attempts to bail out. But his parachute is

in flames. Poor devil! The body somersaults and falls to the ground like a stone.

At an altitude of 3,000 feet there is a tremendous explosion, which causes the spinning fuselage to disintegrate. Fragments of blazing wreckage land on a farm 200 or 300 yards from the Zwischenahn Airfield, and the exploding fuel tank sets the farm buildings on fire.

In a terrific power dive I follow my victim down and land on the runway below. I run over to the scene of the crash. A crowd of people are there, trying to fight the fire in the farmhouse. I join in the rescue work and bring out furniture, animals, and machinery from the burning buildings. Smoke blinds and chokes me, my flying suit is scorched by the flames, as I drag a fat pig out by the hind legs, squealing like mad, from the pigsty, which is completely gutted by the fire. The farmhouse and barns are saved.

Strewn all over a cow field lies the wreckage of the Liberator. The explosion threw clear the crew in mid-air. Their shattered bodies lie beside the smoking remains of the aircraft.

One hundred yards away I find the captain's seat and the nosewheel. A little doll, evidently the mascot, sits undamaged between the shattered windows of the cabin.

One hour later I land at Jever. My men carry me shoulder-high to the dispersal point. That was my fourth combat victory, on my one hundred and sixty-fourth operational mission, and one thousand and fourth flight since I started my instruction with Sergeant Van Diecken.

Dieter was credited with bringing down his seventh opponent: it was his second heavy bomber. In addition, Raddatz, Wenneckers, and Dobrick shot down a Fortress each. That means a score of five combat victories for the Flight, as against nil casualties.

I cannot help thinking about the bodies of the American crew. When will our turn come? Those men share in common with ourselves the great adventure of flying. Separated for the moment by the barrier of war, we shall one day be reunited by death in the air.

February 28, 1943

All last night Lieutenant Gerhard and I sat together in my quarters. The Americans keep us bothered. The question is, what are we going to do about them?

Dieter comes up with a brilliant inspiration. Why not try using our own aircraft to drop bombs on the close-flying American formations?

All night long we sit up calculating velocities and trajectories. We both arrive at the same conclusion: that the desired result could be obtained by means of a simultaneous release of bombs from a Flight in close formation above the massed American bombers. This could then be followed up by an attack of a more orthodox character using our existing armaments.

The Messerschmitt 109G is capable of carrying a load of 500 pounds. Thus it could be adapted to use either four 100-pound bombs or a single 500-pound bomb, or even a rack full of small antipersonnel bombs such as I used to drop on the heads of the Ivans in Russia.

We would require a 15-second time fuse. The altitude for releasing the bombs would be 3,000 feet above the enemy target formation.

I report to the Commanding Officer during the morning and tell him of our project. He thinks it is a joke and begins to laugh. When our urgent entreaties convince him that we are serious, however, he agrees to support our project at Division.

In the afternoon, the Commanding Officer having previously telephoned, I fly to Division Headquarters at Stade. General Schwabedissen and Colonel Henschel (who is in command of the fighter pilots) hear what I have to say and agree to help.

I thereupon submit for approval an order for 100 100-pound practice bombs, release mechanisms for every type of bomb, and bomb dollies for loading the aircraft. I also request the use for one hour every day of a target-towing aircraft, preferably a JU 88, from the Air Servicing Command. This aircraft, with a speed approximately equal to that of the Fortress, is required to tow a ten-foot drogue for us to use as a practice bombing target.

No time is lost in putting my plan into operation. Colonel Henschel himself does not leave the telephone until all arrangements with the Regional Air Command (*Luftgaukommando*) have been completed for obtaining the necessary equipment.

We are going to make use of every opportunity during the next few days for perfecting the precision of our formation flying.

March 8, 1943

Forty-eight hours after my visit to Division Headquarters three heavy motor trucks arrive with the practice bombs. The remainder of the equipment reaches us this morning.

Meanwhile the Flight is kept busy with formation flying practice every day. All my pilots are capable and experienced, and we soon acquire high proficiency. We are able to fly wing tip to wing tip, steady as a board in the air. Every maneuver is executed with smartness and precision, including landing by Sections in formation.

For operational purposes I am on detached duty from the Squadron, which was assigned a few days ago for exclusive use as a tactical unit in operations against the massed enemy formations. I even have my own "Y" control.

In the evening Dieter and I drop our first practice bombs on the drogue target towed by the JU 88. First results are far from satisfactory.

March 10, 1943

Today we spend the entire day at bombing practice on the range at Zwischenahn. I am delighted with the results.

March 12, 1943

The first of the live bombs have arrived. The Flight is now ready for its new task.

March 16, 1943

The mechanics all work hard, practicing bombing-up the aircraft at top speed. They are tremendously keen on the job, and I am delighted by their enthusiasm. They are really good lads.

March 18, 1943

During the morning Dieter and I each drop four of the 100-pound practice bombs on the drogue. My third bomb scores a bull's-eye.

Without any warning at 1412 hours operation orders arrive. We are to attack and intercept a formation of heavy bombers approaching the coast. The order to take off comes so quickly that there is no time for the aircraft to be bombed-up.

Before Dieter closes his canopy he calls over to me that he

wants to bag the enemy formation leader today. I ask him, laughing, if the Yanks have recently taken to painting the wings of their planes with rank badges.

At an altitude of 25,000 feet we establish contact with the enemy in the Heligoland area. I lead the Flight in close formation for a frontal attack.

I open fire on a Liberator from a little below. It immediately starts burning and sheers off to the right as it falls away from the formation. I come in again to attack from above the tail, and then turn for another frontal attack, firing from ahead and below the steeply diving Liberator. My aim has never been better. Suddenly there is an explosion, and the blazing crate disintegrates into a shower of wreckage above my head. For a few minutes I am in danger of collision with falling engines or spinning, flaming wings. That would mean certain disaster for me. Acting quickly, I slam the stick hard over into the left corner and go into a power dive. The falling fuselage of the Liberator misses me by inches as it hurtles into the depths. It falls into the sea some 12 miles southeast of Heligoland.

That was my number five.

I climb back to 25,000 feet for another attack at the massed enemy formation. Suddenly my heart almost stops beating.

Dieter is in the middle of the Yank formation holding his aircraft steady following the same course. His first Liberator went down a few minutes ago. Now he wants to put the formation leader into the North Sea. The lad seems to have gone out of his mind. He keeps hard on the tail of a Fortress, blazing away at it. Tracers from every side converge upon his plane.

He must have become completely insane.

I dive down through the formation toward Dieter, firing indiscriminately at any of the Fortresses flying in the vicinity.

Then Dieter suddenly breaks away in a steep dive. Three thousand feet below, his crate begins emitting a trail of smoke. He opens his canopy, then pushes himself up awkwardly in his seat, and the next moment is thrown clear. His parachute opens. I fly past close to him. His face contorted with pain, he grips his body. Dieter is wounded.

Fifteen minutes later he is down in the sea in map reference sector U-R-9. He succeeds in getting himself clear of the parachute, his rubber dinghy inflates, and he drags himself into it. I fly down low over his head and wave to him. He does not respond. He appears to be either unconscious or in utter pain. It looks as if he has been shot through the stomach.

I immediately report by radio the position of our downed comrade and request help for him. Then I fly in and land. The mechanics look shaken at the news. I find no pleasure in my own success.

If only Dieter is rescued alive. . . .

Alone I fly out to sea again. The others have not yet returned. I can no longer find Dieter. One of the crash boats patrolling the vicinity will have noticed his parachute descent and hurried to his assistance.

Night falls. Still no news of Lieutenant Gerhard.

In his clothes locker I find a bottle of brandy. There is another such bottle in my own locker. We have once agreed that these bottles are to be drunk by the boys in memory of whichever one of us should first fail to return from a mission. What can have happened to Dieter?

At midnight the telephone in my quarters rings.

Lieutenant Dieter Gerhard was found by the crash boat *Falke*. He is dead.

Slowly I replace the receiver. Dieter is dead. He was my closest friend.

I remove the bottle from the locker and go across to Lieutenant Frey. He is in his quarters with his wife and Lilo. They also have been waiting anxiously for news of Dieter. There is no need to say anything.

I pass the bottle to Frey: "Come on: we may as well drink it up. We all feel the same—but that is the way we arranged it with Dieter, and that is the way it has to be."

March 19, 1943

They have brought Dieter in to Cuxhaven and laid out the body in the mortuary at the hospital there. I have had a large wreath made. My men place it in a Fieseler Storch, in which I am going to fly alone to Dieter.

My route crosses the Jadebusen and the broad estuary of the Weser. The water glistens like a mirror, smooth and calm, with the reflection of the rising sun stretching in broad bands of silver to the horizon. Over to the north lies the open sea, from which they brought in the body of my dead comrade.

I land in a small field near the hospital and carry my wreath across to the tiny chapel. There, in the middle of a cold little whitewashed room, Dieter lies under a shroud.

Someone draws it back. The fine, tall lad lies cold and still. It is as if he were asleep, resting the strong body in exhaustion after the effort of that last battle and the final plunge. His eyes are closed, his features in an expression of something resembling defiance.

Good night, Dieter. You have earned your rest, after fighting and dying for our beloved German fatherland. You were my best friend: I shall never forget you. Alone now, I shall continue fighting in this great battle for Germany, which we both started, you and I together, faithful to the same oath of service which we both have sworn.

March 22, 1943

1424 hours. Alert sounds.

Damn! Once again there is no time for our aircraft to be bombed-up. The Americans are coming in from over the sea. They have assembled as usual in the same map reference sector Dora-Dora off Great Yarmouth.

Seven minutes later we receive orders to land. The enemy have turned about and are now heading back in a westerly direction. Will they return?

After landing, the aircraft are refueled immediately, with the pilots standing by. Another alert must be anticipated. The intentions of the enemy are never obvious, as they are in the habit of altering course all the time.

I have a 500-pound high-explosive bomb slung at top speed under my plane. But in the meantime we are ordered to take off, and I am not yet ready to go.

"Flight Sergeant Wenneckers is to take over command." I have the word passed down the line of aircraft.

Wenneckers waves his hand. He has understood, and rolls down the runway. The others follow. The Flight leaves the field in close formation.

Sweating mechanics work feverishly under the belly of my Gustav. I remain strapped in my seat, fuming with impatience.

"Come on, come on; hurry, hurry!"

The Flight disappears, climbing in the direction of the sea. The Yanks have crossed the coast of Holland.

"Ready!"

My weighted plane rumbles awkwardly down to the far end of the runway. With the bomb I cannot take off down-wind.

Turning at the perimeter of the field, my aircraft suddenly lists heavily to port.

A tire has burst.

I fire off a red signal flare. My men over at the Flight dispersal point have understood. Twenty or 30 of them pile into a truck, which comes racing over to me. The left wing is lifted up on powerful backs, and the wheel is changed in a matter of seconds, with the engine still running.

"All clear!" They scatter. I open the throttle, start rolling with gathering speed, and then the crate again begins to list to port. I manage to pull it off the ground, however, after a run of some 600 feet, and clear the roof of No. 2 Hangar by a few inches.

I climb at full throttle up into the cloudless sky, heading out to sea. Overhead are the vapor trails left by our own aircraft and the Yanks. They are already engaged in combat.

22,000 feet: my plane reacts sluggishly under the infernally heavy load. It climbs wearily up to 30,000 feet, taking 25 minutes to do so.

The Yanks have bombed Wilhelmshaven, as I can tell from the smoke and fires below. They are over Heligoland on the return flight now.

I edge forward slowly until I am over the tip of the enemy formation, which consists entirely of Fortresses. For several minutes I am under fire from below, while I take a very rough sort of aim at my target, weaving and dipping each wing tip alternately in order to see the formation below. Two or three holes appear in my left wing.

I fuse the bomb, take final aim, and press the release button on my stick. My bomb goes hurtling down. I watch it fall and bank steeply as I break away.

Then it explodes, exactly in the center of a row of Fortresses. A wing breaks off one of them, and two others plunge away in alarm.

Twenty miles west of Heligoland my third heavy bomber crashes into the sea. There is no sign of fire. It is followed by the torn wing fluttering down like an autumn leaf.

The bomb has registered a hit. Not only on the Fortresses, but also, it seems, on our own higher brass.

Immediately after landing I am ordered to report to the Commanding Officer of the Wing *(Kommodore)*. He himself was in the air at the time, and observed the crash of the Fortress.

"Good Lord, Knoke, you must do that again with your whole Flight!"

"That is my intention, sir."

"Do you believe that it will work?"

I am not too certain. "Today could have been just a fluke, sir; but perhaps we can bring down some more of the heavy babies this way."

Then Colonel Henschel telephones. "I am delighted, my dear Knoke. That was a magnificent job. Must congratulate you." He bleats away happily and sounds quite worked up. I hope his monocle will not fall into his cup of cocoa in the excitement.

The North Sea coastal area of Germany must have its little sensation!

Least fuss is made in the Flight. I find all this excitement over bringing down one single bomber rather absurd. First, anybody could have dropped the bomb. Second, the original idea was not mine but Dieter's. Third, I have eight holes in my own plane where it was hit.

During the night I am awakened by the telephone ringing at my bedside. It is the station switchboard.

"Sir, there is a top-priority call for you from the Air Force High Command (OKL)."

"What! For me?"

I give my name.

A Major is at the other end, on the Staff of Reich Marshal Göring. "You brought down an enemy aircraft today by bombing it, did you not?"

"Yes, sir."

I am asked for complete details: What type of bomb? What kind of fuse? How exactly had I carried out the attack? And just what had been the result?

"Who issued the order for this bombing operation?"

"No one, sir. I acted on my own initiative."

There is a silence. For the first time it occurs to me that I was never authorized to lay so much as an egg on the head of the wretched Yank, and so they might consider that I had acted in an exceedingly high-handed manner.

Then the Major comes back on to the line:

"I am putting you through to the Reich Marshal."

This is the shock of my life!

I lie rigid, stiffening in bed to a horizontal position of attention, to report: "Lieutenant Knoke, No. 5 Flight Commander, No. 1 Fighter Wing."

"I am delighted over the initiative you have displayed. I want personally to express to you my particular appreciation."

And that is that.

So there we have a full-fledged Prussian Lieutenant in the German Air Force talking to his Commander-in-Chief while lying in bed wearing nothing but a pajama jacket. Incredible!

If the Old Man only knew! I am not even wearing the

trousers: the tight elastic irritates me. I cannot help laughing at the thought as I turn over again.

March 23, 1943

When I arrive on duty out at the dispersal point there is a message from the station switchboard: "Sir, last night there was a call from the Experimental Station at Rechlin. They ask you to let them have a full report immediately."

Good God! If only I had never dropped that bomb!

At 1000 hours General Kammhuber calls. This poisonous little twerp, commonly known as "Wurzelsepp," is Commanding General of the Twelfth Air Corps.

I receive a terrific reprimand on account of my high-handed action of yesterday. He is incoherent with rage. I have to hold the telephone at arm's length from my ear until the din subsides.

"Where do you suppose we would get to if every Lieutenant just did as he damned well pleased?" shouts the irate voice at the other end. "What the hell do you think you were doing?"

I knew that question was coming. It happens every time in our services whenever the superior officer runs out of his store of expletives when administering a reprimand. Am I expected to answer that I cannot help playing with bombs because I so adore the funny noise they make when they go off?

"Well, do you have anything to say for yourself?"

I most certainly have!

"Yes, sir. Last night the Reich Marshal telephoned me and personally expressed his appreciation of my initiative."

There! That takes care of Wurzelsepp. I hear him deflate with a gasp. One man's meat is another man's poison, according to the old German proverb.

Colonel Lützow, the Inspector of the German Fighter Command, arrives by air during the afternoon.

The tall, young Colonel is one of our finest fighter pilots, his decorations including the Knight's Cross with Swords. He is popular with all ranks because of his easy charm and warm personality. In an entirely simple and straightforward way he discusses with me the potentialities inherent in air-to-air bombing operations.

As an experimental measure it is decided that one of the Flights in No. 26 Fighter Wing, based on the Channel Coast, shall also attempt to bomb the massed Yank formations. We both are convinced that in any event these tactics cannot last long, once the enemy provides the bombers with an escort of fighters.

"What an unholy uproar there has been over that wretched egg, sir! It makes me wish I had never dropped it!"

Lützow laughs: "Me, too!"

April 17, 1943

The Americans made an attack on Bremen today. We take off with our bombs, which we have a chance to drop when the Flight is in close formation over the heart of Bremen. Not a single bomb registers.

We immediately go in to attack with our guns. I make three runs at a Fortress, and it finally catches fire. Southwest of Bremen, in a field near Bassum, it crashes. Four members of the crew parachute to safety.

The Flight is credited with three more victories.

May 14, 1943

The enemy raids Kiel. We go after him again with our bombs. Several times I attempt a formation attack 30,000 feet above Holstein. Every time the enemy formation weaves out of the way below. Apparently they have guessed our intentions.

Over Kiel we run into heavy flak from our own guns. The shooting by the Navy is unfortunately so good that we are considerably disorganized.

I observe the Yank bombing. They dump their load right on the Germania Shipyards. I am impressed by the precision with which those bastards bomb: it is fantastic.

My chance of bringing off a formation drop has gone by now, so I send the Flight in one at a time.

My own bomb fails to explode. Hits are registered, however, by Flight Sergeants Führmann and Fest and Sergeant Biermann. Three of the Fortresses are destroyed in mid-air.

Once again relying on my guns, I dive for a frontal attack against a detached formation of some 30 Fortresses.

Almost at once I feel a hit in the fuselage, and as a result I have to abandon the attack. My engine continues running smoothly, however, and all the controls seem to be working.

I attempt another frontal attack. My first salvo registers right in the control cabin of a Fortress. It rears up, like a great animal that has been mortally wounded, and drops away in steep spirals to the right. At approximately 10,000 feet a wing breaks off. It crashes near Husum at 1217 hours.

I get home with several holes in my fuselage and tail.

Today my Flight has shot down five heavy bombers. The total Flight bag credited has now reached 50 heavy bombers, and the fiftieth was brought down by Flight Sergeant Wenneckers. Thus my No. 5 Flight is now credited with shooting down as many heavy bombers as the Squadron Headquarters and No. 4 and 6 Flights all together.

During an inspection of the Squadron later in the afternoon General Galland, General Commanding the German

Over Wangerooge Sergeant Kramer also is hit. With his tail shot away and out of control, he collides in mid-air with Sergeant Biermann. The two aircraft are locked together for several seconds and drop almost vertically. Then Biermann somehow gets his badly damaged plane clear, and brings it gliding down to the airfield. He attempts a deadstick landing, but his speed is too great and he overturns. The aircraft is totally destroyed and Biermann is—uninjured.

Kramer bails out. He loses his nerve and tries to open his chute while traveling at a speed of more than 400 miles per hour. Two of the harness straps break. The chute is half open when he hits the sea. He is rescued spitting blood and is taken to hospital.

June 11, 1943

The Yank does not come over again until this evening.

Twice we take off to intercept. Only on the second mission, when the formation is far out to sea heading for home, does my chance to fire come. One of the Fortresses finally goes down after my fourth run at it.

June 13, 1943

Today is the thirteenth of the month.

The flight carries out a formation attack on a batch consisting of some 120 heavy bombers. There is a Fortress beautifully lined up in my sights. I press both firing buttons and—nothing happens. I check my magazine loader and safety catch, press the buttons again, and—still nothing happens.

Seething with rage, I spiral down into the cloudbank below.

Today is the thirteenth!

June 25, 1943

I am still feeling like death when I come crawling out to the dispersal point this morning. The other pilots and I all stayed in the canteen until daybreak. The bar is littered with a whole regiment of empty bottles.

The sky is overcast. We hope that this is going to be one day the Yank will leave us in peace. In the Squadron operations room no enemy activity is reported. I lie down to catch up on some sleep in the restroom adjoining the crew room.

The telephone wakes me at 0700 hours: enemy concentrations in map reference sector Dora-Dora.

As if they could not choose some other day!

The pilots are still asleep. I do not disturb them but go outside to the aircraft. The chief engineer reports all aircraft checked and found serviceable.

Going into the dining room, I order a fried egg and some white bread and butter, which I try to eat. The food seems to be quite tasteless. For the first time I do not feel happy at the thought of the coming mission. There is a peculiar sinking feeling in the pit of my stomach. Is it fear?

No, I do not think it is fear exactly, so much as disinclination and indifference. Even a visit to the can fails to bring relief. I spend 15 minutes running up and down the runway, trying to pull myself together. Turit, my dog, trots alongside. Now and again he dashes off, barking after a sea gull.

From the operations room comes the order to stand by for an alert. The pilots are yawning as they come out one by one. After they have had something to eat, they crawl into fur boots, flying suits, and life jackets. There is little talk. I stuff some emergency rations and a first-aid kit into my capacious knee pocket.

Slowly we stroll across to our aircraft. The alert is due at any moment. The mechanics are there before us. My ground-crew chief dangles his legs as he lolls along a wing, chewing a blade of grass. What a picture of alertness!

Arndt fastens my harness as I put on my helmet. He passes me the ground telephone extension. The Commanding Officer is on the line.

He asks if we are all set. The Flight Commanders answer in turn: Lieutenant Sommer, myself, and Captain Falken-samer. The enemy is approaching the coast: apparently today he is again heading for Wilhelmshaven.

0811 hours. Take off.

The Flights take off in succession, 44 aircraft in all. The cloud ceiling is at 6,000 feet. We pass through it when we are over the coastline. Occasionally we catch a glimpse of the earth through gaps in the clouds.

15,000 feet: another cloud layer is crossed in our ascent.

20,000 feet: there is no conversation on the radio. Only the enemy positions are announced.

22,000 feet: we may expect at any moment to sight the enemy.

I check my guns. My oxygen mask feels unpleasantly tight. I loosen and adjust it.

We fly between cumulus clouds. High above us spreads a third layer of ice clouds. We fly through valleys and caverns, across gigantic mountains of cloud. Our planes seem absurdly small, dwarfed by this majestic background.

"There they are!"

The Fortresses are nearly 3,000 feet below us. They are not flying in massed formation today, but make their way, singly or in groups of threes and fours, through the magnificent cloudscape.

Peeling off, we go down diving.

"After them!" The chase is on.

June 25, 1943 113

It is a perfect surprise. Our attack throws the Americans into a state of utter confusion. They dodge and turn and dive for cover in the clouds as they try to get away from us. It is impossible to estimate how many of them there are. It is just as if a beehive was overturned. We call out to each other the best firing positions by radio.

In pairs our pilots attack the individual groups of Fortresses. As my wingman today I have a young Sergeant with me for the first time. This is his first experience of air combat. There is a good chance that it may be also his first victory, if he keeps his head.

I select two isolated heavy bombers flying wing tip to wing tip, and we go down to attack them from the rear.

"Dölling, you take the one on the left."

I call the Sergeant; but he keeps flying away off to the right and does not heed my call.

"Close in, man! Other side—over to the *left*! Get in and attack!"

I open fire at short range. My cannon shells land beautifully in the center of the fuselage. The rear gunner persistently returns my fire. I calmly close in, guns blazing. Holes appear in my right wing as I am hit. That bastard of a rear gunner! He will not leave me alone—must have a lot of guts.

Closer still I keep on blasting away at the Fortress, concentrating on the rear turret. It disintegrates under the salvos from my cannon. More high explosive puts the dorsal turret out of action also.

We are between clouds, in a deep ravine, with milky walls towering high on both sides. It is a glorious picture. Dölling still keeps flying obstinately in his position to my right, calmly watching the shooting. Why does he not go after the second heavy bomber?

I lose my temper with him now: "Attack, you bloody fool, *attack!*"

He still makes no move.

Woomf! Woomf! Woomf!

I am under heavy fire from the side. It comes from the right side turret of the second Fortress. I am in a position close alongside. The dorsal gunner also blazes away at me with his twin guns. Tracers pass close by my head.

Woomf! I feel another hit. We pass through wisps of cloud. My windows fog up, so I slide open the side window.

My Fortress is on fire along the back and in the left inside engine. Still the two gunners in the second Fortress keep on blazing away at me. They are only 100 feet away.

I continue firing at my victim. The bastard has got to go down, even if it means my own neck. I remain 150 to 200 feet behind his tail. The fire now spreads to his right wing.

I drop the stick for a moment and try to attract the attention of Dölling by waving and pointing to the second Fortress. There is a sudden flash in front of my eyes, and I feel my waving hand slammed violently against the right side of the aircraft. Alarmed, I reach for the stick, but drop it again immediately. My right glove is in shreds, with blood trickling out. I do not feel any pain.

Once again I grasp the stick with my injured hand, line up the sights on my opponent, and empty the magazine in one long burst. At long last the Fortress goes down, falling into the clouds like a flaming torch.

I go down after it, following as far as the sea. There, all that is left of the heavy bomber is a large patch of oil burning on the surface.

By now my hand is starting to hurt. I take the stick in my left hand and find it smeared with blood. Shreds of flesh hang from the torn glove.

I lost my bearings some time ago during the shooting above the clouds. Heading south, however, I am bound to reach land somewhere. It is a miracle that my engine has not been hit. By a stroke of good luck the gunners on that Fortress were not good marksmen.

The pain in my hand is getting worse. I am losing a lot of blood. My flying suit looks as if I had been wallowing in a slaughterhouse.

How far out at sea can I be? Minutes drag by; and still there is no sign of that damned coastline. I begin to have a peculiar hot, sickly sort of feeling: must be getting light-headed.

This pain in my hand!

An island looms up ahead: Norderney. Only seven or eight minutes more, and then I can land. The time seems interminable. Finally I am over Jever. In spite of the throbbing pain in my hand I dive low over the Flight dispersal point and announce my success with a victory roll.

The mechanics wave their hands and caps, as delighted as children. And now I need both hands for landing. I grit my teeth. My right hand is completely numb.

My ground-crew chief is horrified at the sight of my hand and the blood over my flying suit. The mechanics swarm round my aircraft. The Chief has been wounded!

At the station first-aid post Medical Officer on duty removes the glove and places an emergency dressing on my hand. I also receive a precautionary antitetanus injection.

It is only 0900 hours. The last of the aircraft do not return until noon. Two more victories can be chalked up on the scoreboard at the dispersal point.

At noon I am finally taken to the hospital. They have to operate. One finger joint is amputated. The hand will be all right otherwise, unless gangrene sets in.

A nursing sister takes me into a ward. I am supposed to remain there until further notice. I look outside: my car is still there in the courtyard below. Jungmaier, my driver, has waited.

Cautiously I peep down the long corridor. The coast is clear: no one is in sight. I never could stand the smell of disinfectant in hospitals. Half an hour later I am back at my Flight dispersal point.

I cannot help laughing: they may be looking for me at that hospital to this day, for all I know.

July 2, 1943

It had been my intention to remain with the Flight; but the Commanding Officer, Captain Specht (who assumed command of the Squadron two months ago), ordered me to take a few days' leave, and together with Lilo and little Ingrid I went to Hamelin.

Three and a half years have passed since I left home. Then I had just taken my senior matriculation and was wanting to become a soldier. Now I am back as a Senior Lieutenant—I was promoted a month ago and confirmed in my appointment as Flight Commander—having been awarded the Iron Cross First and Second Class, the black wound stripe, and the pilot's insignia. During the last few months, too, I have received operational wings in bronze, silver, and gold, for having completed more than 200 missions.

In those days I was in love with Annaliese, and today I am a married man and a father, too.

In our dear old rat-hole nothing has changed.

Every day the dressing on my hand is changed at the local hospital. I have my arm in a sling. Somehow I cannot help feeling rather proud of my first wound.

July 4, 1943

I am still supposed to have almost another week of leave. I find, however, that I miss the airfield, the comrades, and the planes, so I decide to return.

Furthermore, I cannot possibly imagine the Flight being able to carry on without me!

July 25, 1943

I have a sort of leather shield made to protect the bandage on my right hand, and I am able to fly again with the help of a looped strap attached to the control stick.

I have put in a lot of flying during the last few days in a Messerschmitt Taifun, a smart-looking four-passenger aircraft.

Today I flew over the city of Hamburg. The British by night and the Americans by day in a series of massed air attacks have practically destroyed this great city. Entire sections of the city have been devastated by nightly British phosphorus incendiary bombings. The death toll is estimated at 100,000. The Americans cover objectives of military importance by day.

During my flight I observe the great fires that are still raging everywhere in what has become a vast area of rubble. A monster cloud of smoke rises up to 3,000 feet above the fires, fanning out to a width of some 10 to 20 miles, as it slowly drifts eastward to the Baltic Sea, 70 miles away.

There is not a cloud in the sky. The giant column of rising smoke stands out starkly against the summer blue. The horror of the scene makes a deep impression on me. The war is assuming some hideous aspects.

I resolve with grim determination to return to operations in spite of my wounded hand.

July 27, 1943

During a test flight I learn that I am able to fly my Gustav by inserting my hand into a leather sling fitted over the stick.

In the afternoon I go up with the Flight for a practice flight. I shall have to avoid dogfights with enemy fighters, on account of my hand; but I shall be able to manage attacks on the bombers.

Unfortunately during this practice flight Sergeant Kramer crashes into the sea—only a few days after coming out of hospital—as a result of engine trouble. We see him go down, but are unable to help. The aircraft vanishes forever into the North Sea.

July 28, 1943

Concentrations in map reference sector Dora-Dora. That means action. I shall strap my hand to the control stick and fly.

We take off with 11 aircraft at 0835 hours. Bombs have been slung under the bellies.

In the Heligoland area we climb over the approaching bombers and release our bombs. A fantastic scene is produced by the explosions.

The close-flying formation is disorganized completely. Some of the Fortresses plunge down in steep dives, while others swerve off to the sides. They narrowly escape mid-air collision. The bomb dropped by Sergeant Fest has exploded exactly in the center of a close flight of three heavy bombers together. All three simultaneously go down to crash. More than 20 parachutes float in the air.

Our earphones resound with whoops of triumph. This is something terrific. We loop and roll above the enemy formation in sheer joy, and it is several minutes before we settle down again. To think that Jonny Fest should have been able to bring down three of the monsters at a single blow! Several of the others have obviously been damaged.

I shout encouragement over the radio to my men: ". . . and now let's give them the works!"

We dive in formation right into the Yanks. My men are completely carried away. Earphones scream with calls from every side: "After them! After them!"

We continue our onslaught until we are close enough to the Fortresses to ram them. I have a new aircraft with a 30-mm. cannon. It punches great holes in the fuselage of the Fortress which I have picked as my victim.

Alarmed, the pilot tries to get away by plunging. Five or six more of the enemy, some of them on fire, also swerve away from what remains of the battered formation. Now we can pick them off one by one! One after another they go down in flames to crash into the sea. Only large patches of burning oil remain on the surface.

What a chase!

When I have brought down my opponent, I return to the attack on the disrupted formation. Together with Flight Sergeant Raddatz I open fire on another Fortress, until it is in flames. Raddatz finishes it off, when it tries to escape to the west.

Then I observe that one of the comrades is on fire. Opening my throttle, I draw alongside. It is Sergeant Höfig.

"Take it easy, Höfig! Just keep cool!"

The long flames spread down his fuselage.

"Bail out now, Höfig, if you don't want your hide roasted!"

I call to the others to remain absolutely calm. Kramer would not have drowned yesterday if only he had kept his head.

Then the body of the Sergeant falls clear of the burning plane. He is caught by the slipstream and tossed high into the air. For 5,000 to 10,000 feet he falls like a stone, then opens his parachute.

I follow him down, circling his parachute. Höfig waves his hand, then points downward. The sea awaits him below.

I radio a call to base for help: "Little brother shot down in Ulrich-Quelle-six. Parachute descent into sea. Notify rescue service."

Base acknowledges my call. They will pick up Höfig. For a long time he drifts through the air, before finally landing on the surface of the water.

Ten aircraft land undamaged at 0950 hours. The mechanics carry us shoulder-high from the aircraft over to the dispersal point. They are completely overjoyed.

Arndt, my ground-crew chief, offers his congratulations and for the sixth time makes me a ceremonial presentation of the same pot of flowers:

> I certainly do save a lot,
> Always presenting the same old pot!

The flight is in a state of wild enthusiasm. Pilots everywhere stand surrounded by the soldiers and tell the story. Eleven victories to be added to our score on the board. Eleven heavy bombers will drop no more bombs on Hamburg.

The rescue service will be busy fishing half a company of Americans out of the sea. And Höfig will be taking a cold dip, in company with his colleagues from the other side.

In the evening a rescue service aircraft brings him over from Heligoland, where he had been landed with a crashboat load of Yanks. He is in high spirits, unhurt except for a slight burn on his forehead.

Practically overnight he traded his Boy Scout uniform for this one of Hitler's *Jungfolk*. Age: 18.

Cockpit of a Messerschmitt: from 1940 to 1944, this virtually was his home.

(*Courtesy of* Flying *magazine*)

A German observation plane follows the action against a Spitfire . . .

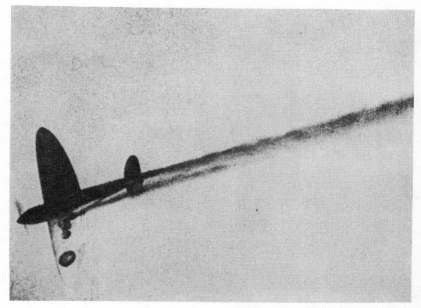

. . . and a few seconds later Knoke is credited with another kill.

(*U. S. Army Air Force Photo*)

When the "heavy babies" started coming over unescorted by fighters, Knoke and members of his Fifth Squadron saw hundreds of scenes like this (note Liberator crew member bailing out) . . .

(*U. S. Army Air Force Photo*)

. . . and this: a B-17 Flying Fort going down in flames over target,

The Messerschmitt 109E: Knoke's introduction to the dangers and difficulties of this machine was a fearful ordeal, but he went on to master it, found that it could outmaneuver most of its foes.

The Focke-Wulf 190: until the middle of 1943, these and the Messerschmitts ran up a lopsided score against the Allies' bombers.

Pilots of the "Fifth *Staffel*," or Squadron, Knoke in the center, in the summer of 1943. Only five of them lived to celebrate Christmas.

On the plane's tail, between the swastika and Knoke, are 9 small vertical marks, one for each U. S. bomber.

Here is North American's P-51 Mustang. Its speed and the fire power of its four cannon caused the Germans a great deal of trouble.

An echelon line-up of Republic's P-47 Thunderbolts: as swarms of these began escorting the bombers, the hunters became the hunted.

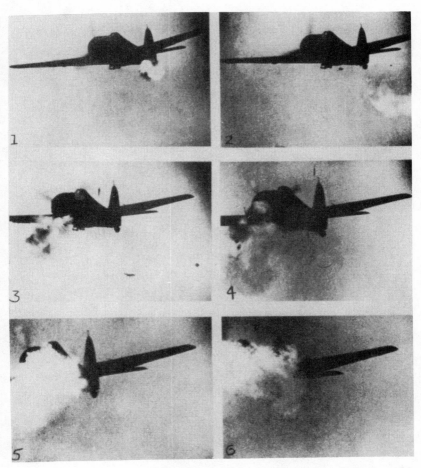

This could have been Knoke himself. These photos, taken by a camera gun on an RAF Typhoon, show the split-second stages of disintegration of a Focke-Wulf 190. The pilot reported: "Once I had him nicely in my sights I went right in, pressing my gun button all the way." Knoke would have appreciated that remark.

Major Specht turned his missing
eye away from the camera's lens.

Compare this 1943 photograph of Knoke with the one at the beginning
of this section in which he is wearing the uniform of the *Jungfolk*.
Five years and a rough war can do a lot to a man's face.

"Boy, oh boy, what a shooting party!" is all he says, when the comrades welcome him back.

Jonny Fest, of course, is the hero of the day. He is credited with bagging three heavy bombers on a single operation.

Telephone calls arrive from the other Flights. They have observed our attack, and call to congratulate us on its success. I am really proud of "my Fifth." In my own logbook I enter the thirteenth on my score.

This day will remain in our memories as the great "shooting party."

August 15, 1943

Once again "my Fifth" is detailed for a special assignment.

Our aircraft are rigged under each wing with objects whose strange appearance causes them to be given the name of "stovepipes." These are, in fact, ejection tubes for a kind of eight-inch mortar shell, or rather a rocket, consisting of a propellant charge, an explosive charge, and a time fuse. At this rate we shall soon find ourselves carrying heavy artillery.

The idea seems to be for our Flights to form up at a range of 2,500 feet behind the enemy formations, and then use the contraptions for firing explosive rockets at them.

August 17, 1943

There is a surprise in the early morning, when we are suddenly transferred to Rheine, some 120 miles to the south. Heavy attacks by American formations are anticipated on central Germany. We are to operate in conjunction with the Wings already stationed in that sector.

After only 90 minutes, however, further orders come for us to transfer to Gilze Rijn, in Holland. We land there at 1115 hours.

I cannot coax it to Hangelar. I dare not take a chance on that engine again.

6,000 feet . . . 5,000 . . . 3,000. I pick out what looks like a large field, and spiral down toward it. The ground comes rushing up at a terrific speed.

I prepare for a belly landing, and once again switch on the ignition. The engine starts. I have to make tighter turns in order to reach the landing field. Suddenly the engine begins to grind and clatter to a standstill for the last time. Cut!

It has seized. The prop is rigid, held as if by a vise. My plane becomes heavy and unresponsive to the controls. It begins to stall, and the left wing drops.

Damn!

I push the nose down hard and regain control. Houses flash past below in a nearby village. My airspeed indicator registers 200 miles per hour. I almost scrape the tops of some tall trees below.

150 miles per hour: I must touch down.

120 miles per hour: my wing tips scrape the treetops.

The indicator registers 100 miles per hour. I smash through two or three wooden fences. The splintering posts and cross-bars fly in all directions. Dust and chunks of earth hurtle into the air. I hit the ground, bounce, bracing myself for the crash hard against the safety belt, with feet clamped on the rudder pedals. A dyke looms ahead. Holy smoke!

C—r—ash!!!

And then a deathly silence. I unfasten the safety belt and drag myself out of the seat. My Gustav looks like an old bucket which has been well kicked around and trampled underfoot. It is a total wreck. There is nothing left intact except the tail-wheel.

Blood oozes from my right sleeve.

August 18, 1943

The Squadron rescue patrol Weihe aircraft was kept busy all day today collecting our pilots who were shot down. We call it the flying garbage truck.

My return to Jever at noon is greeted with loud cheers. There were some shrapnel fragments in my upper right arm. The Medical Officer at Hangelar removed them last night.

August 19, 1943

In future our aircraft are to be equipped with extra reserve fuel tanks, in order to increase their range. The Squadron is detailed for operations over central and southern Germany.

The Gustavs in my Flight are becoming sluggish to handle under the heavy load of stovepipes as well as everything else that has to be carried.

September 27, 1943

Enemy concentrations in map reference sector Dora-Dora. Once again the time has come. . . .

1030 hours. Stand by.

1045 hours. All set. I have a new aircraft. Arndt has been polishing it until it shines like a new mirror: no doubt that will add another ten miles per hour to the speed.

1055 hours. The call to action blares as usual from the loud-speakers round the field: "All Flights take off! All Flights take off!"

The sky is completely overcast. We come out above the clouds at 10,000 feet and at the same moment sight our Fortresses directly overhead. We climb on a parallel course, heading east up to 20,000 feet. That is as high as they are flying today.

The reserve tanks are still almost full when I order my Flight to jettison them. We swing quickly in to attack with our rockets. As we get into position, the Fortresses split up into separate groups of some 30 or 40 aircraft each, and keep on constantly altering course. The moisture trails above the cloudbank leave a zigzag pattern in the blue sky.

I order all our rockets discharged when we are in formation at a range of 2,000 feet. The next moment a simply fantastic scene unfolds before my eyes. My own two rockets both register a perfect bull's-eye on a Fortress. Thereupon I am confronted with an enormous solid ball of fire. The bomber has blown up in mid-air with its entire load of bombs. The blazing, smoking fragments come fluttering down.

Wenneckers also scores a direct hit. His victim goes down in flames.

My wingman, Sergeant Reinhard, has discharged his rockets to explode beside another Fortress. The fuselage appears to be damaged, too, and it swerves away off to the left. I observe how Reinhard chases off merrily after it, blazing away with his guns. He fastens on to the tail of the American.

My attention just then is attracted by the rather peculiar appearance overhead of double moisture trails, apparently emanating from very fast aircraft. What can they be? Only Messerschmitts and Focke-Wulfs, as far as I know, have been sent into action from your side. The peculiar-looking planes keep circling above the bombers. If they are German, why do they not attack?

I climb up alone for a closer look at them. Lightnings! Twelve or 14 aircraft: the Yank has brought a fighter escort. I radio the warning to my comrades. Since I cannot undertake operations against them by myself alone, I decide to swoop down once more upon the Fortresses.

Then suddenly four other peculiar-looking single-engine aircraft dive past. They have the white star and broad white stripes as wing markings. Damn! They are Thunderbolts. I have not seen them before.

I immediately dive down after them. They swing round in a steep spiral to the left, heading for a lone Flying Fortress whose two outside engines have stopped. There is a Messerschmitt on its tail: it is Reinhard.

The bloody fool has eyes only for his fat bomber and is unaware of the enemy fighters coming up behind.

"Reinhard, Reinhard, wake up! Thunderbolts behind!"

Reinhard does not reply but keeps on calmly blazing away at his Fortress. I go flat out after the Thunderbolts. The first of them now opens fire on my wingman. The latter just keeps on firing at his victim.

But now the leading Thunderbolt is a perfect target in my sights. A single burst of fire from my guns is all that is needed. It bursts into flames and goes down spinning like a dead leaf into the depths below. It is my second kill today.

Then there is a sudden hammering noise in my crate. I turn round. There is a Thunderbolt hard on my tail, and two others are coming down to join it. I push the stick right forward with both hands, diving for cover in the clouds.

Too late: my engine is on fire. I can feel the heat: it quickly becomes unbearable.

Jettisoning the canopy, I pull the oxygen mask off my face. I unfasten the safety harness and, drawing up my legs, kick the stick forward with all my strength. I am shot clear out of the aircraft and somersault through the air in a great arc. I feel the flying suit whipped against my body by the rush of wind.

Slowly I pull the rip cord. The harness cuts in, and I am pulled up with a jerk as the parachute opens. After the terrific drop I seem to be standing on air. I swing gently from side to side. Overhead, the broad, white silk parachute spreads out like a sun awning. The supporting shrouds make a reassuring "whoosh." I quite enjoy the experience. What a marvelous invention the parachute is, to be sure—always provided it opens!

Jever lies off to the north. They must be able to see me from there. If they only knew that this is the commander of the "Fifth" who is now dangling ignominiously because of having allowed himself to be outmaneuvered by a Thunderbolt. I come down in a field, after dropping the last few feet in a rush.

Time: 1126 hours. Only 31 minutes since I was airborne. Time enough for three aircraft to have been brought down. It is some consolation, however, that the score is two to one in my favor.

Arndt, my faithful ground-crew chief, sees me come back with the parachute underneath my arm. His face drops. "That lovely Gustav!" he moans, sadly shaking his head.

It is black day indeed for the Squadron. By evening it is ascertained that among my own pilots Sergeant Dölling has been killed, and Raddatz and Jonny Fest shot down also. Fest is wounded, in hospital at Emden. No. 4 Flight has lost two killed and one seriously wounded.

One of the Headquarters aircraft has not returned.

No. 6 Flight seems to have got the worst of it. Nine out of its 12 pilots are lost. All of the nine have been killed. The remaining three have been forced to either crash-land or bail out. Not a single one of their aircraft returned.

On the credit side, however, we have brought down 12 of

the enemy to offset these heavy casualties. No fewer than six are credited to my lucky "Fifth" alone.

My own score has now risen to 16.

The heavy casualties on our side are to be explained by the fact that nobody had anticipated an encounter with enemy fighters. We were taken completely by surprise.

Added to the credit side, of course, there is also the fact that today the Americans failed to reach their objective. They were obliged to take their bombs back home with them. The only exception was one of the smaller formations of Fortresses. They unloaded their bombs through a hole in the clouds on the little town of Esens in East Friesia. A school was hit, and 120 children were killed—that was one third of the entire child population of the place.

This war has become a merciless affair. Its horrors cannot be escaped.

October 2, 1943

We have been transferred to Marx, a large operational air-field with concrete runways, south of the Jever station.

Our first mission from here is a failure. First, we are unable to establish contact with a formation of Fortresses which turned out to sea; and second, one of the pilots in No. 4 Flight crashed in the dirty weather and was killed.

October 4, 1943

From early morning our listening stations report intense aerial activity over southeast England. The weather is good. It is expected that the Americans will come over. The reports received so far, however, fail to give a clear picture of what is happening.

We sit out in front of the hangar. The loud-speakers play us gay music.

The Senior Warrant Officer comes over to me with a folder bulging with a lot of papers. This blasted paper war makes me sick. I glance quickly through them, initialing the most important. My thoughts are far away, already considering our coming tangle with the Fortresses.

Turit chases off down the runway, barking angrily after some sea gulls which have flown in from the sea. Yesterday I took him rabbit hunting. He is a splendid hunting dog, alert, intelligent, full of life, and exceptionally fast.

The music from the loud-speakers suddenly fades: "Attention, all Flights! Attention, all Flights! Stand by for take-off."

Mechanics come pouring out of the hangar and run over to the aircraft. The pilots follow. Turit sits on my left wing as I fasten the safety harness. He fondly watches with his intelligent, brown eyes. Ever since the time I brought him back with me from Norway, he takes his position on the wing whenever I am about to fly. Only after the engine has started does he allow himself to be blown from the wing by the air pressure. Then he runs along behind the aircraft taking off, until outdistanced.

Arndt passes me the ground telephone extension.

Flight Commanders report to Captain Specht. He explains the situation to us. The Americans are approaching over the sea off the north of Holland. Today, for the first time, we are to try making a frontal attack in close Squadron formation of more than 40 aircraft.

At 0932 hours orders to take off are given by Division. Flight after Flight leaves the field, wheeling to the left and circling to take up position in the assembling Squadron formation.

"Follow course three-six-zero," orders base.

Slowly we climb. Radio silence is seldom broken. At 22,000 feet our engines begin leaving long moisture trails.

It is cold. Breath freezes on the oxygen masks in front of my mouth and nose. At intervals I have to slap my thighs vigorously in order to keep warm.

And now we sight the enemy, a formation of some 300 or 400 heavy bombers, far in the west. The Commanding Officer swings round toward them.

A few minutes, and we are tearing into the enemy with every gun blazing. I head full speed for the nose of a Liberator. Fire! Duck away sharply beneath the giant fuselage to avoid a collision, keep on going right on through the formation, pull up hard in a climbing turn to the left, and then round back again.

My salvo has had its effect. The Liberator swerves, drops out of the formation, and heads away in the opposite direction.

"No, my friend, that is not the idea! You are not to go home now."

As soon as my Liberator is separated from its brethren and beyond the range of their guns, I close in under the fat belly and continue firing until it is in flames. The Liberator burns very much faster than the more streamlined Fortresses. Eight men immediately bail out. The parachutes mushroom in the air and hang there swaying.

The heavy crate glides away down. I draw up alongside and stay within 60 to 100 feet of it, certain that no living soul can still be aboard. I can distinctly see the great holes punched by my cannon shells in the nose and tailplane.

Suddenly I notice the flashes in the dorsal turret. Too late! A salvo of fire smashes into my crate. My engine bursts into flames at once. There is no response when I move the controls.

Once again it is time for me to hit the silk, jettison the canopy, unfasten the safety belt. My plane stalls, plunges, rights itself again, . . . and then I am thrown clear as if by some giant hand. . . .

Somehow my parachute must have opened, although I do not remember pulling the rip cord. Several hundred feet below I observe the other parachutes. This is one time the Americans and I go bathing together.

It seems to me that the water comes up the last few feet with a rush. I press the quick release on the harness just as I go under. It is cold—bitterly cold—and salty.

I have no sooner come to the surface than a foaming breaker crashes over my head, and I am left spluttering for air. My life jacket inflates. It carries me up the crest of a high wave. On the other side I am tossed down into a deep green valley.

My rubber dinghy appears to be all right, too. When half inflated, it is almost torn right out of my hands by another breaker crashing down. In a dip between the waves I finally succeed in heaving myself into the bouncing rubber boat.

Wave after wave rolls past. Every second one has an angry crest of white foam, and I am choked and blinded. Up and down we heave and roll, up and down, up and down, in a monotonous rhythm. Wave after wave pounds and batters at my tiny coracle. Water pours in faster than I can bail it out.

I rip open my little bag of dye, and watch it spread through the surrounding water, tingeing it a sickly yellowish-green and slowly permeating my flying suit with the same color.

The comrades have observed my descent. I have absolute faith in my eventual rescue from here. If only it were not so cold and this perpetual rocking up and down would only stop. I look at my watch. It has stopped. And it was supposed to be waterproof.

When I bailed out it seems my right knee pocket was torn. The packet of emergency rations has gone, also my Very pistol seems to have been wrenched out of the holster. I unfasten my belt with the signal flare cartridges attached, and throw it away. What use is such ballast to me now?

The sky overhead is still streaked with moisture trails. The formation has disappeared long ago into the east. I do not know how long I have been sitting in my cold salt bath.

An aircraft comes heading in my direction from the south. I wave like a madman. They have got to see me; they have got to get me out of here. I have no desire to drown like a mangy dog.

It is a Focke-Wulf Weihe—a rescue service aircraft. It comes down low over my head, and I am able to make out the crew. They wave to me and swoop down again. A bundle drops from the rear turret. It inflates as it falls. A rubber raft.

Because I am so intent on watching the rubber raft drop, I fail to notice a breaker, and so I am nearly thrown out of the dinghy. I swallow a lot of water and begin to choke. Yet another breaker crashes over my head. The water tastes horribly salty.

The Weihe continues to circle encouragingly overhead. I see the raft just ahead. I can reach it by swimming a few yards. It seems to take a long time for me to muster enough strength to pull myself up into the tightly inflated raft. Then I can only flop down in a state of complete exhaustion.

For perhaps two hours I lie there on the raft, tossed by the waves in a never-ending rhythm up and down, up and down. Then the bow of a crash boat looms in sight. Strong arms lift me on to the deck. Saved!

Huddled in a woolen blanket, I am landed on Heligoland, and a rescue service Weihe flies me back to Marx.

October 5, 1943

I am suffering from a hell of a hang-over today. Last night I was with the pilots, celebrating somebody's birthday. It was a shambles! The crew room today looks like the morning after a battle.

In the afternoon I take off with four aircraft on a sea-rescue search. Yesterday it was I who lay down there on the waves. Today we are looking for survivors from a ship which went down after hitting a mine.

There is a haze and dense fog out to sea. We return to base after searching for an hour and a half without success. Once again the sea has taken its toll. I am fortunate to have escaped from its clutches.

October 8, 1943

Today I make the following entry in my logbook:
Date: Oct. 8.
Take-off: 1422—Marx.
Landing: 1521—Marx.
Flying time: 59 minutes.
Remarks: Bomber formation with fighter escort intercepted over North Holland. Shot down one Fortress south of Dollart.

October 9, 1943

After having yesterday won my eighteenth combat victory, I am obliged today to break off an air combat with Fortresses over Flensburg without further success.

My propeller pitch-control mechanism is hit. The prop feathers for gliding, and remains in that position, so that I am forced to turn off the engine, and have to go down for a deadstick landing at the airfield on Westerland Island.

October 10, 1943

The Yanks do not leave us alone. Today they attack Münster in strength. Just when I am ready to pounce with my Flight on a formation of Fortresses over the burning city, we are intercepted by Thunderbolts.

A wild dogfight begins. The Thunderbolt has a clumsy appearance which is belied by its high speed and maneuverability. It can still be outfought, however, by a Messerschmitt in the hands of a good pilot.

During the dogfight I observe a Messerschmitt 110—one of the aircraft from No. 76 Fighter-Bomber Wing—firing four rockets into a group of Fortresses. Two of the Fortresses explode in mid-air. Thereupon, several Thunderbolts come swooping after the victor. Warrant Officers Barran and Führmann and I dive to intercept them.

At my first burst of fire a Thunderbolt ahead of me blows up, and Führmann shoots down a second one. That brings the entire pack of Thunderbolts down on our necks. It is all we can do to shake them off. I try every trick I know, and put on quite a display of aerobatics. Finally I get away by spiraling up in a corkscrew climb.

I know that the Thunderbolt cannot duplicate this maneuver. Unfortunately neither Barran or Führmann is able to keep up with me. They are still in a serious predicament, with ten or 12 of the Yanks on their tails, and in the meantime the fighter-bombers have got away.

Choosing my time, I return diving into the *mêlée* alone once again, firing at random to divert the attention of our pursuers from Barran and Führmann. In doing so, I am badly hit in the tailplane and left wing where the undercarriage lies retracted.

The crate flips over onto its back and plunges down vertically. I am unable to bring it under control again. This infernal dive continues down to 3,000 feet. It is a hell of a sticky situation. I break into a cold sweat all over, and my hands begin to shake. "Knoke," I think to myself, "this time you have had it!"

In utter desperation I try pushing the stick over to the side. It has jammed. I take my feet off the rudder pedals, and as a last resort kick hard against the stick. Suddenly there is a violent jolt, my head is banged hard against the side window, and—the plane is back again in a normal flying position.

Barran has dived down with me, but from sheer terror he has remained speechless on the radio.

At Twente I put my aircraft down in a belly landing beside the runway. Half the tail was shot away, and also the right leg from the undercarriage.

Shortly after me a Focke-Wulf comes down to land on the runway. A leg breaks as it touches down on the concrete, it overturns and bursts into flames. The pilot is trapped in his seat and burns to death in front of my eyes before he can extricate himself. I am powerless to help: I have to watch him being slowly cremated alive in the wreck. I am trembling at the knees.

A few minutes later a shower of bombs from a formation of heavies comes down close to the airfield.

I have had enough for one day.

November 17, 1943

On October 14, November 13 and 15, we are sent into action against formations of heavy bombers over the Rhineland; but no further successes are won by the Flight. Every time, we become involved in dogfights with the escorting Thunderbolts, Mustangs, and Lightnings.

This morning the pilots from three of the fighter and fighter-bomber wings are drawn up for inspection on parade at Achmer. Reich Marshal Göring appears in a motorcade of approximately 30 vehicles. My conversation with him lasts for about ten minutes, when the most successful of the Fortress specialists are personally presented to him.

At the moment I happen to be leading in the Division Area, with a score of 15 heavy bombers. Captain Specht and Senior Lieutenant Frey are second and third, with 14 and 12 respectively.

Göring makes a most peculiar impression. He wears a unique kind of fancy gray uniform. His cap and epaulets are covered with gold braid. Bulging legs emerge from scarlet boots of doeskin. The bloated, puffy face makes him look to me like a sick man. Close up, I am forced to the conclusion that he uses cosmetics. He has a pleasant voice, however, and is extremely cordial to me. I know that he takes genuine interest in the welfare of his air crews.

Göring asks about the enemy aircraft I have shot down. He is particularly interested in my first Mosquito last year. He well remembers the occasion. In his opinion the Mosquito aircraft is nothing but an infernal nuisance and pain in the neck. He reiterates this with emphasis. The two which raided Berlin then caused him particular annoyance because he was starting an important public speech at the time, and had been forced to postpone it for two hours on account of the raid.

He personally awards me the German Gold Cross.

The Reich Marshal subsequently addresses us, discussing the problems involved in the defense of the Reich and the extraordinary difficulties which must be faced. It is a surprise to us when he expresses the opinion that it is we, the air crews assigned to the defense of the Reich, who must be held responsible for the failure of air defenses in the West.

He refers to the magnificent effort of the fighter pilots of the Royal Air Force in the Battle of Britain and commends their courage as a shining example to us. With this part of his address I am completely in agreement. It seems to me, however, even as he speaks, that the Commander-in-Chief of the German Air Force has actually only a vague idea of what happens when we engage in combat with the strong American formations.

The inescapable fact is that on the technical side our performance is inferior in every respect. The victories in Poland and France resulted in the High Command of the German Air Force simply going to sleep on its laurels. The number of defense units operating under the general scheme of air defense of the Reich is altogether inadequate for the task. The numerical superiority of the enemy is in the ratio of at least eight to one.

Such successes as are still being achieved in the face of these overwhelming odds are due simply and solely to the excellent morale and fighting spirit of our air crews. We need more aircraft, better engines—and fewer Headquarters.

November 19, 1943

Yesterday, after an unsuccessful attempt to intercept an approaching Yank formation, we landed late in the evening at St. Trond in Belgium.

The weather closed in. Holland and Belgium lay banketed by a murky overcast and swept by heavy blizzards. Through a gap in the clouds we climbed up to the usual altitude for operations. Inside the cloudbank there was a serious risk of icing. It stretched like a vast expanse of white blanket northward as far as the sea. Our good Messerschmitts were sparkling in the sunshine. From the Daimler-Benz engines the exhausts traced long trails of moisture across the brittle cold of the pallid autumn sky. On our oxygen masks the frozen breath congealed.

So we headed north in close formation, just like migrant cranes. Base reported the approach of a strong formation of Fortresses coming in over the sea. One of the planes—it was Führmann—gradually fell behind the formation and began losing altitude, as if overtired after the long climb.

To my radio inquiry he answered that he was having trouble with his engine. Over this sort of murk anyone let down by his engine has no alternative but to bail out, if he values his life. The Flight Sergeant was in luck, however. His engine did not die altogether, and after we were airborne for an hour the mission was abandoned because the enemy bombers turned back. Thunderbolts would have blasted his limping crate like a sitting duck.

Through a friendly gap in the clouds I was able to bring my Flight down safely to St. Trond.

Erich Führmann was the last to land, and his aircraft rolled unsteadily across the worn turf at the end of the runway. Light snow had begun to fall, and that is rather unusual here at this time of year. Even before we manage to thaw the chill out of our bones round the stove in the wooden canteen hut, our planes outside are coated with the congealing snow, until they look like petrified monsters out of some fairy tale.

When Führmann came in to join us an hour later, we were sitting in a noisy group with steaming glasses of hot rum punch. His engine was all right again: the trouble had been found in the supercharger. By that time we had started the inevitable game of cards, and also emptied several glasses of the strong and heartwarming beverage.

Führmann at first did not want to join in the noisy gambling game. He merely shrugged and held out his hand, rubbing thumb and forefinger together. He never had any money. Somebody dragged him up to the table and pressed him into a chair. Somebody else tossed him two shining five-franc pieces. Many things must have played their part in the life of Erich Führmann; but at the end of his life the strangest part of all was played by those two five-franc pieces.

Erich began to play, and—something which had never happened before—he won. He increased his stake and won again. He kept on winning with incredible certainty. He took over the bank, and still he won. We were staggered. Hours passed. A thick cloud of blue tobacco smoke hung down from the low ceiling. Empty bottles and glasses were carelessly tossed aside to litter the floor.

I watched Führmann.

He was posted to my Flight several months ago. He became one of our comrades. The sky was his element. Like the rest of us, he felt at home there. With all its many changes of mood, the sky gives us a sense of remoteness from the war-torn battlefields of Europe over which we flew.

Together with the rest of us, he became passionately addicted to the life of a fighter pilot, the combination of intense joy in flying and the thrill of battle. Because he also shared our sense of patriotism, he became a good soldier as well as a good pilot.

For him, as for us, the wonderful fact of flying and the spirit of chivalry which still exists in battle far above the clouds resulted in a sense of unrestricted happiness and peace of mind. The ever-present prospect of sudden death adds a zest to life while it lasts. Dedicated as we are to the serious business of fighting for our country, we are able to enjoy the mere fact of existence with a superb exhilaration simply because it is so uncertain and precious. We regard life as a jug of delicious Rhine wine, intoxicated by the sense of compelling urgency to savor every last drop while we can, draining it to the dregs in an atmosphere of companionship and gaiety.

When we were not in the air Führmann was always to be found somewhere around the station, in the hangars, canteen, or at the dispersal point. He was simply always there. Nobody paid him any particular attention. If he was away, there was just a vague feeling that something was missing. He was background personified. He rarely opened his mouth, and even when he did nobody listened to what he said.

Once when we were discussing our comrade and how quiet he always was, one of the numerous girls on the station remarked that still waters run deep. She was smiling to herself at the time and probably knew what she was talking about. . . .

As the game finished, the noisy high spirits at the start had been superseded by a tense silence. Führmann continued winning to the very end. Then he contentedly placed in his shabby old wallet six 100-mark notes and with a loving smile added the two five-franc pieces.

Then he quietly withdrew to his customary place in the background.

At noon today we started on our return flight. The weather was unchanged.

When we landed at our home station Führmann was no longer with us. Once again he had dropped far behind. His

That thing which sank into the northern moor, that thing which was fished out of the sea, those shattered remains on the rocky crags—they have nothing in common with our memories of Führmann, Dieter, Dolenga. . . .

"Fellows, do you not think they would die laughing at the sight of our gloomy faces down here? You can bet that old scoundrel Führmann is just waiting for the next one to join him to start another card game."

It was Jonny Fest who spoke. His humor is irrepressible.

"It makes me sick," growled Methuselah.

His motto is: "Swearing is the laxative which purges the soul." He has already written it beneath his portrait, in case it, too, has to join the others on the wall.

December 11, 1943

On November 26 and 27 and December 1, we engaged in combat with American fighters over the Ruhr and Rhineland.

Today I brought my score up to 20. It was another Fortress.

December 18, 1943

For three days I have been supposed to go on leave, but I have not yet managed to get away.

The Americans come over every day. Yesterday I was actually sitting in the car which was supposed to have driven me to the train when the alert sounded over the loud-speakers. I jumped out and ran across to my Gustav. My driver shook his head, and even Arndt said that I really needed a few days' rest.

At an altitude of 10,000 feet I have to abandon the mission because my undercarriage would not retract. Wenneckers took over command. They shot down two Fortresses and a

Thunderbolt. It looks as if they will somehow be able to manage without me, after all.

Today I am off. Jungmaier drives me to the railway station. Standing on the platform, I watch the Squadron sweeping in to action once again.

For a long time I am able to watch them from the window of the moving troop train. For the first time in almost a year I am not accompanying them.

December 20, 1943

Lilo and I are again in Berlin. We thought of having some fun there for a few days, visiting old friends and seeing the opera and latest shows.

We hardly recognize Berlin: it is so changed. Hundreds of thousands of foreigners pack the city—Dutch, French, Danes, Belgians, Romanians, Bulgarians, Poles, Czechs, Norwegians, Greeks, Italians, Spaniards. Every language in Europe is to be heard in the overcrowded cinemas, theaters, cabarets, restaurants, metropolitan railway trains, and streetcars. Everywhere they push aside the Berliners. Lilo and I are unable to get a seat anywhere.

The confused babel of languages and the crowds of people wherever we go make me jittery. People here live as if there was no such thing as war anywhere in the world. Our life on operations may be basic and primitive, but at least it is real. That is something we soldiers understand out there, as we risk our very lives every day in the great life-and-death struggle. It is a shock to find that here in the city people are interested only in their own selfish amusements. This typical base area is governed by a thoroughly civilian mentality, blind to the fundamental realities to which we on operations are accustomed.

I see the staff officers who are stationed in Berlin, sleek, well groomed, immaculate in their dress uniforms. I have been living too long in a different world and have developed a different scale of values. The atmosphere of this place makes me sick.

December 22, 1943

Together with Ingrid we have gone to visit my parents at Schieratz. Here at home with my family I at last begin to find a little peace. With a horse and sleigh I go for long drives through the wintry countryside along the banks of the Warthe.

Lilo and I are happy to be together. Ingrid is a pretty little curly-head, and I find it good to be here. Even so, I rather miss my comrades and the airfield, the smell of the planes, and the roaring engines.

December 26, 1943

Another Christmas has come and gone. War still reigns upon the face of the earth.

Early this morning a telegram comes from the Squadron: "FALKENSAMER KILLED—SOMMER WOUNDED—SPECHT."

The Commanding Officer drafted it himself. He has not ordered my leave canceled or an immediate return to the unit; but I understand how badly he must need me now, with Captain Falkensamer, who was in command of the "Fourth," killed and Senior Lieutenant Sommer, who was in command of the "Sixth," wounded. I am the only Flight Commander he now has left who is fit for operations.

Two hours after receiving the telegram I am on the first train out. Lilo understands. She is brave, as only a soldier's wife can be. She stands waving and smiling as the express begins to move.

Will we ever meet again?

December 27, 1943

I traveled all day and night. Jungmaier met the train at Wunsdorf. He drives me the last few miles out to the airfield. The Squadron was transferred here a few days ago. It is a well-equipped peacetime station, most up to date in its construction.

I report immediately to the Commanding Officer: "Senior Lieutenant Knoke reporting back from leave, sir."

Specht smiles as we shake hands: "I knew you would not let me down, Knoke. I really need you now."

He tells me how Falkensamer was killed. I am distressed about this first-rate officer. Immaculate in appearance, tall, slim, he was popular and had an easy social charm of manner. His home was in Vienna, and he had previously served in the Austrian Air Force. His father had been an Imperial officer in the First World War. He had a particularly charming wife, whom Lilo and I had met at Jever a few months ago.

Falkensamer was very tall; but Specht, who is now seated in front of me in his leather flying suit, is short. He is actually the shortest man in the whole Squadron. Yet all who have any contact with the man are impressed by his dominating personality.

Of all the officers I have met, none has influenced me to quite the same extent. Specht is a model of the conscientious Prussian soldier. He is as hard on himself as on his subordinates and expects them to maintain the same Spartan ideal of conduct which he exemplifies.

He lost an eye during a dogfight at the beginning of the

war. With his one remaining eye he looks like a buzzard. All that matters to Specht is battle. His only topics for conversation are Fortresses, Thunderbolts, Mustangs, and Lightnings. Once he dragged me out of bed in the middle of the night simply to discuss some tactical problem.

Women are an anathema to him. He has forbidden his officers to bring any of their wives or girl friends on to the station. If he spots a pilot out with a girl of questionable reputation, he takes immediate and stern disciplinary action.

During the last ten months he has shot down 20 heavy bombers and thus is now ahead of me. His accuracy as a marksman is positively uncanny.

He is a most difficult Commanding Officer, and I have had many a row with him. A few weeks ago he reprimanded me because some of my pilots organized a party and went dancing at a village inn near the airfield with a number of girls who were better known for their charms than for their morals. He ordered me to take disciplinary action against my men.

I refused to do so: "I cannot do that, sir."

"Then you are not fit to command a Flight," he roared. The little man was wild with rage.

"In that case, sir, you will have to find a new commander for the 'Fifth.' "

"I shall have you relieved of your command and all your pilots grounded."

"May I remind you, sir, that during the last few months, which have been difficult for all of us, more enemy aircraft have been brought down by my pilots than by the other two Flights and your Headquarters put together."

I know that Specht has actually a very high opinion of "my Fifth"; but nothing will ever induce such a reserved man to admit as much.

In spite of his capricious temperament, however, I have a deep respect for him. Unquestionably he is a great man.

December 31, 1943

We had planned a party in town on New Year's Eve. At 1700 hours, however, the order came from Specht that no officer or air-crew personnel might leave the camp. Instead they were ordered to attend a Joint Mess Dinner in the officers' mess. Specht had never been cursed so much as he was following the announcement of this order. When we enter the mess at 2000 hours we are all in high spirits. Several bottles of liquor have been emptied to drown our sorrows.

Specht calls us to attention and briefly explains the reason for his order: "Gentlemen, I have received word from Division that an important decision is to be made tonight. In order that the maximum operational efficiency of the air crews may be maintained, I have decided to forbid the usual New Year's Eve celebrations. We shall spend the remaining hours of the old year here together and retire to bed immediately after midnight."

He spoke in his usual ringing voice of command. What each of us thought we kept to ourselves.

At midnight precisely the momentous news arrives from Division. Specht is promoted to Major!

He is absolutely staggered. He had expected some special operational assignment for the Squadron. Amid loud cheers, he immediately dismisses the pilots. In a few minutes none of them is left in the mess.

6

January 1, 1944

My men are sleepy and suffering from hang-overs when they appear at the dispersal point. I heard them return singing from town in the small hours of the morning. My own head is splitting also. All day long we can only hope that just for this one day the Yanks will not come over.

1944 is off to a liquid start.

January 4, 1944

For nearly a week the Fortresses have left us in peace. Today the concentrations are again reported in sector Dora-Dora.

At 1002 hours the Squadron takes off for the first mission of 1944. Over Münster we run into fire from our own flak as we attack a strong formation of Fortresses.

Closing in to attack one of several separate groups, my aircraft is caught by a direct hit. It immediately becomes tail-heavy. The roar of the engine turns into a high-pitched wail and then into a grating screech, and finally all is silent. One of the flak shells has shot away my propeller, cowling, and the front part of the engine. It is all I can do to hold the aircraft under control.

Next moment a Thunderbolt comes diving at me and shoots up the wing which bursts into flames. He does not have a second chance to attack me, however, before Wenneckers puts an end to his career with a burst from his guns.

It is only by exerting all my strength that I am able to hold the stick at all. I must bail out before being overcome by the flames. Jettison the canopy, unfasten the safety belt! I know the routine now.

Before I am ready, however, I am jerked out of the seat by the slipstream. I am left dangling. My parachute is caught in the baggage compartment, which has somehow come open. I am stuck with my right leg outside and my left leg still inside the cockpit.

My plane is practically over on its back and plunging with increasing speed toward the earth. I am unable to move. The terrific force of the slipstream keeps me glued to the back of the fuselage. It whips at my left leg scrabbling in the air and almost twists it off. I am screaming with pain. It whips at my cheeks and plugs my nostrils. The pressure is such that I can scarcely breathe. The flames are licking across my body.

The aircraft begins to flutter, then goes into another spin, practically vertical. I cannot even move my arms in the terrific wind pressure. If I do not somehow get clear of the aircraft it is the end!

I have to get clear . . . get clear . . . get clear. . . .

I fall some 10,000 . . . 12,000 feet. With a final herculean effort, which brings blood streaming from my nose, I succeed in hooking my right foot round the stick. I push hard over to one side. The plane half rolls, hesitates, seems to stand on its tail, and hovers for a moment as it loses speed —and then I am clear! For a split second I am sailing through the air alongside the fuselage. Something hits my back a terrific blow, and I feel as if I were cut in two. Then a second blow on the head knocks me out completely.

I have no idea what happened after that.

When I come to, I am in the clouds under my open parachute. The rip cord is still in the socket, so I suppose it must have opened by itself. I am fighting for breath, but cannot get any. An attempt to shout produces only an agonized groan.

Suddenly the ground appears. The cloud ceiling is only 600 feet. My parachute swings wildly from side to side. Almost horizontal, I hurtle low over the roof of a house and land heavily on the solidly frozen ground in the garden.

Then I lose consciousness again. The next thing I know, I am in an ambulance.

In hospital at Münster I am examined and X-rayed. Diagnosis: skull fracture, fractured lumbar vertebræ, severe bruising of shoulders and right pelvis, local wound under right hip, severe brain concussion, temporary paralysis of right side owing to spinal displacement.

I vomit continually. Orderlies carry me into a ward with a large window and lift me into a newly made bed beside the wall. I am in great pain and wish that I could sleep.

And today was to have been the last day of my leave with Lilo and little Ingrid. . . .

It is evening before I again become capable of any sort of coherent thought.

A Senior Lieutenant from Bomber Command is in the bed opposite. We introduce ourselves. He has lost his right leg and left foot. It was a direct hit by flak in Russia.

January 30, 1944

Twenty-six days have passed since I was wounded. I could

not stand being confined in the great hospital, with its eternal odor of disinfectant, and requested transfer back to the first-aid post casualty ward at Wunsdorf air station. Here I can at least be with the Flight again.

Every morning I was carried out to the dispersal point, where I would spend the day lying in a deck chair wrapped up in heavy blankets.

Those must have been the days which caused the hair of our Squadron Medical Officer to turn white. Contrary to his strict orders, I would persist in getting up and trying to walk. At first my paralyzed limbs gave a lot of trouble. Then there was noticeable daily improvement. In time I became accustomed to the never-ending headaches.

This morning brought operation orders for transfer to Holland. We are to be based at Arnhem for action against the heavy bombers. On crutches I hobble over to my Gustav and accompany the others. Specht is surprised but not displeased to see me there when I report to him after landing.

At 1305 hours we take off again.

Emerging above the clouds, we are attacked immediately by Spitfires. We are taken completely by surprise, and we cannot put up effective opposition to the Tommies. They drive us off in a wild chase. It is a case of every man for himself. I never once have a chance to fire. We suffer heavy casualties.

Near Hilversum my engine is hit and knocked out. I am lucky to be able to set my crate down in a crash-landing on its belly a mile from Hilversum airfield.

Specht is the only one of us who succeeds in shooting down a Spitfire. No. 4 Flight has lost five killed, No. 6 has lost three, and Headquarters has lost one. I have lost from my own Flight (No. 5) Sergeant Nowotny, who was posted to me only a few weeks ago.

Raddatz is dead. That is a heavy blow for the Flight. Raddatz had been with the Flight ever since its formation. I never met a more brilliant pilot. He was the finest of comrades. I cannot believe that he is in fact no more.

February 11, 1944

Today over Mainz we had a wild dogfight with American fighters, who were escorting their Fortresses. We landed at Wiesbaden between engagements.

February 20, 1944

The Squadron had two long engagements today with formations of Fortresses over north Germany and the North Sea.

Specht was forced down and had to make an emergency landing on the Danish island of Aroe.

Bad shooting on my part caused me to miss a good opportunity of adding to my score.

February 21, 1944

Today I flew two more missions. We had orders to draw off the escorting fighters at any cost and keep them engaged in combat with us. Other Squadrons meanwhile attacked the heavy bombers. That cost my Squadron two more dead.

February 22, 1944

1254 hours. Take off to intercept. The Americans are approaching central Germany. I am able to take only five aircraft into the air, as losses suffered by the Squadron during recent weeks have been very heavy.

More than 1,000 enemy aircraft are reported. The Americans no longer fly in massed formations; but come over in groups of 30 or 40 at a time. The route which they follow we call the "bomber alley." These bomber alleys are carefully guarded by the vigilant fighters.

Today the bomber alley happens to pass directly over my old home town, Hamelin. By a strange chance I go into action directly over the familiar hills and mountains just west of Hamelin. Accompanied by Corporal Kreuger, who was posted to the Flight only two days ago, I attack a Fortress in a formation of about 30 heavy bombers.

An automatic camera has been attached to my guns for the past two weeks. The resulting films are to be used for training purposes in Fighter Schools. In a frontal attack on the heavy bomber I place my first salvo directly in the control cabin. I come in again, this time diving down upon my victim from above the tail until a collision is imminent. The Fortress tries weaving out of my line of fire and swerves sharply round to the left. Yet my shells continue to plaster the left wing and left side of the fuselage.

I cannot help thinking of my camera. The films of this engagement, when enlarged, may prove to be really instructive. Flames come belching out of the tail. I pull in close beneath the monster fuselage and continue blasting away with all I have in the magazines.

The young Corporal, by this time, has taken on the Fortress off to my left. The lad has lots of guts, pressing his attack to within a few feet of the enemy and not flinching, although severely hit.

Then the crew of my Fortress bail out. The fuselage is a blazing torch. It makes a wide sweep round to the left and begins to go down, its passage marked by a long trail of black smoke.

Hamelin is directly below.

The blazing Fortress dives ever more steeply, and soon it

is in a vertical spin. It crashes in a pasture beside the river at the south end of my old home town. A tower of flame spurts high into the air. The pasture directly across the river was the one from which as a boy I had taken off for my first flight during that air display so long ago.

At that moment a second aircraft comes hurtling down out of the sky. It crashes in a lumber yard at the south end of Hamelin, on the premises of the Kaminski wagon-manufacturing and repair workshops. It was my wingman, the young Corporal. This was his first mission.

I swoop low over the flaming wreckage, but he was killed instantly. In a wide sweep I fly low over the rooftops of my old rat-hole. The streets are deserted. All the good citizens of Hamelin are no doubt sitting timidly in their cellars and shelters.

With my last drop of fuel I land again, after 90 minutes, at Wunsdorf.

A second time I take off after the Fortresses when they are homeward bound. I do not have another chance to fire at any of the bombers, however, because I have to spend half an hour in a dogfight with a whole pack of Thunderbolts. They seem altogether too eager to catch me with my pants down.

February 24, 1944

During the morning I receive news that on one of the most recent night operations Geiger also has been killed. Only a few weeks ago he was awarded the Oak-leaf Cluster to the Knight's Cross and promoted to Captain. Out of the little group of pupils of Van Diecken at the Military Academy, I am now the sole survivor. Hain and Menapace were killed in Russia a few weeks ago.

The Squadron loses another six killed at noon today in a

dogfight with Thunderbolts, Lightnings, and Mustangs covering another heavy bombing attack.

Our little band grows smaller and smaller. Every man can work out for himself on the fingers of one hand when his own turn is due to come.

February 25, 1944

The Americans and British conduct their large-scale air operations in a way which leaves us no respite. They have rained hundreds of thousands of tons of high explosive and phosphorus incendiary bombs upon our cities and industrial centers. Night after night the wail of the sirens heralds more raids. How much longer can it all continue?

Once again Division Control reports those blasted concentrations in sector Dora-Dora. It is the daily waiting for the action call, the permanent state of tension in which we live, which keeps our nerves on edge. Every mission is now followed by some more pictures going up on the wall.

Concentrations in sector Dora-Dora! This report has now come to have a different significance for us: it is a reminder that, for the moment, we are still alive. The faces of the comrades have become grave and haggard.

Concentrations in sector Dora-Dora! Today it will be the same story again. In silence we prepare for take-off. One by one we again retire into the can. That is also part of the same routine. No laxatives are needed to assist the sinking feeling Dora-Dora creates.

Take-off at 1600 hours.

The Squadron circles the airfield until it is assembled in formation.

"Climb to 25,000 feet on course due north," calls base. "Heavy babies approaching over the sea."

At 15,000 feet over Lüneberg Heath we are joined by the Flights from our Third Squadron. It is cold. I turn on the oxygen.

20,000 feet: we maintain radio silence. Base periodically gives the latest enemy position reports, "Heavy babies now in sector Siegfried-Paula."

22,000 feet: we fly strung out in open formation. The monotonous hum of the code sign is in our earphones. Di-da-di-da-di-da-di-da . . . short-long-short-long-short-long. . . .

25,000 feet: our exhausts leave long vapor trails behind.

30,000 feet: my supercharger runs smoothly. Revs, boost, oil, and radiator temperatures, instrument check shows everything as it should be. Compass registers course three-six-zero.

"On your left . . . watch for heavy babies to your left."

There is still no sign of them. Nerves are tense. I am suddenly very wide awake. Carefully I scan the skies. Vast layers of cloud cover the distant earth below as far as the eye can see. We are now at an altitude of 33,000 feet: it should be just right for bagging a few enemy bombers or fighters.

Vapor trails ahead. There they are!

"I see them," Specht reports with a crackle of his ringing voice.

"Victor, victor," base acknowledges.

The bomber alley lies about 6,000 feet below us—600 to 800 of the heavy bombers are heading eastward. Alongside and above them range the escorting fighters.

And now I am utterly absorbed in the excitement of the chase. Specht dips his left wing tip, and we peel off for the attack. Messerschmitt after Messerschmitt follows him down.

"After them!" The radio is a babel of sound, with everybody shouting at once.

I check my guns and adjust the sights as we dive down upon the target. Then I grasp the stick with both hands, groping for the triggers with my right thumb and forefinger. I glance behind. Thunderbolts are coming down after us.

We are faster, and before they can intercept us we reach the Fortresses. Our fighters come sweeping through the bomber formation in a frontal attack. I press the triggers, and my aircraft shudders under the recoil.

"After them!"

My cannon shells punch holes in the wing of a Fortress. Damn! I was aiming for the control cabin.

I climb away steeply behind the formation, followed by my Flight. Then the Thunderbolts are upon us. It is a wild dogfight. Several times I try to maneuver into position for firing at one of their planes. Every time I am forced to break away, because there are two—four—five—or even ten Thunderbolts on my tail.

Everybody is milling around like mad, friend and foe alike. But the Yanks outnumber us by four or five to one. Then some Lightnings come to join in the *mêlée*. I get one of them in my sights. Fire!

Tracers come whizzing in a stream close past my head. I duck instinctively.

Woomf! Woomf! Good shooting!

I am forced to pull up out of it in a steep corkscrew climb, falling back on my old stand-by in such emergencies. For the moment I have a breathing space. I check the instruments and controls. All seems well. Wenneckers draws alongside and points down at four Lightnings on our left.

"After them!"

Our left wing tips dip, and we peel off. We hurtle down toward the Lightnings as they glisten in the sun. I open fire. Too fast: I overshoot the Lightning. I wonder what to do about my excessive speed.

But now a Lightning is on my tail. In a flash I slam the

stick hard over into the left corner. The wing drops. I go down in a tight spiral dive. The engine screams. I throttle back. My aircraft shudders under the terrific strain. Rivets spring from the wing-frame. My ears pop. Slowly and very cautiously I begin to straighten out. I am thrust forward and down into the seat. My vision blacks out. I feel my chin forced down on to my chest.

A Lightning passes me, going down in flames. There is a Messerschmitt on its tail.

"Got it!"

It is Wenneckers.

A few moments later he is alongside me again. I wave to him with both hands.

"Congratulations!"

"The bastard was after your hide," he replies.

It is the second time Wenneckers has shot a Yank from off my tail.

After we land I go up to Wenneckers to shake hands, congratulate him on his success, and—. But Wenneckers interrupts before I am able to thank him: "No need for you to thank me, sir. I only wanted your wife not to be made a widow by that bastard. Besides, think what a nuisance to the Flight it would have been to have had to dispose of your remains!"

All the mechanics standing around greet this remark with roars of laughter. I dig the lanky lad in the ribs. We go together into the crew room. Meanwhile the others have also been coming in to land. This is one day we all come back.

March 3, 1944

The Americans attack Hamburg. Specht cannot fly, and I am in temporary command of the Squadron. Our original 40 aircraft have now been reduced to 18. These I take into the air.

Over Hamburg I prepare to attack a small formation of Fortresses. My 18 crates are 5,000 feet above them. Just as I am about to dive, I observe, about 3,000 feet below and to the left, a pack of some 60 Mustangs. They cannot see us, for we happen to be directly between them and the dazzling sun.

This is a magnificent opportunity!

I throttle back to allow the enemy pack to get a little way ahead of us. Wenneckers draws alongside, waving and clasping his hands in delight. For once we are in a position to teach them a real lesson, but I must be careful not to dive too soon. They have not spotted us yet. After them!

In a practically vertical dive we hurtle into the midst of the Yanks, and almost simultaneously we open fire. We take them completely by surprise. In great spirals the Mustangs attempt to get away. Several of them are in flames before they can reach the clouds. One literally disintegrates under fire from my guns.

Yells of triumph echo over our radio.

In the evening I receive the report from Division that the wreckage of no fewer than 12 crashed Mustangs had been found in map reference sectors Cæsar-Anton-four and -seven.

There is only one drop of sorrow to tinge the general rejoicing. Methuselah has not returned. Several of the pilots saw a Messerschmitt 109 without wings going down. What has become of Methuselah?

March 4, 1944

News of Methuselah! He is in hospital near Hamburg. A Mustang shot off both his wings, and then his aircraft

exploded. As a result he was injured, but succeeded in parachuting to safety.

Out of all the "old-timers" I now have only Wenneckers
and Fest left with me. The other pilots are all young and
inexperienced and have been with us only since January.

March 6, 1944

Today we have another dogfight with Thunderbolts south
of Bremen.

Early in the afternoon I take into the air for a short test
flight a new pilot who reported on posting to the Flight only
yesterday. While practicing low-level flying he ran into the
ground and was killed.

March 8, 1944

Last night there were more engines droning overhead. The
British attacked Berlin with more than 1,000 aircraft.

At noon we are sent into action against the Americans who
are heading for the same objective. Once again I am in command of the Squadron.

In the first frontal attack I shoot down a Fortress just north
of the airfield and leave a second one in flames. I cannot
watch it crash, however, because I am fully occupied with
several Thunderbolts trying to get on my tail.

My Flight loses Sergeant Veit. The body was found in a
cornfield just north of the airfield where he was shot down.

On our second mission I succeed in shooting down yet
another Fortress. It also went down during the first frontal
attack, aimed at the control cabin. Probably both pilots were
killed and the controls put out of action, because the plane
crashed without any signs of fire.

During the ensuing dogfight with the Thunderbolts my

tailplane was shot full of holes, and my engine and left wing were badly hit also. It is all I can do to limp home to our field. On coming in to land I discover that my left wheel has been shot away. The right wheel will not retract. I am forced to make a one-wheel landing.

As I touch down, there are an ambulance and a fire engine standing by at the end of the runway ready to receive me, but their services are not required. I succeed in achieving a smooth landing.

Immediately I order a reserve aircraft to be prepared for me to take off on a third mission. It is destroyed during a low-level strafing attack. Two of the mechanics are seriously wounded.

No. 4 Flight places one of its aircraft at my disposal by order of the Commanding Officer. Specht and I take off together, with Flight Sergeant Hauptmann and Sergeant Zambelli as our wingmen.

When we attempt to attack a formation of Liberators over Lüneberg Heath, we are taken by surprise by approximately 40 Thunderbolts. In the ensuing dogfight our two wingmen are both shot down. After a wild chase right down to ground level the Commanding Officer and I finally escape with great difficulty.

After landing I receive word from Diepholz that Flight Sergeant Wenneckers is in hospital there after being shot down and seriously wounded.

In a telephone conversation with Division during the night, the Commanding Officer requests that the Squadron be withdrawn from operations temporarily. We cannot continue.

The request is refused. We are to continue flying to the last aircraft and the last pilot. Berlin, the capital city of the Reich, is ablaze from end to end.

Several hundred Thunderbolts and Lightnings came over with more than 1,000 heavy bombers. Jonny and I landed sweating like pigs. Both our aircraft were shot up.

Again we flop into our armchairs. Specht enters the room.

"The Squadron will be withdrawn from operations for six weeks," he announces. "I think we have earned this rest."

Jonny and I can only nod agreement.

As soon as the Commanding Officer has finished his cigarette and leaves the room, I bring out a bottle of brandy from my locker.

Two hours later I produce a second bottle. The first is empty. Jonny and I are alone.

Jonny tells me all about his girl friend at home in Wesel. I tell him about Lilo: she is expecting our second child in a month.

Jonny decides that he wants to have four children, after having first married the girl friend.

"That is, of course," he murmurs to himself as an afterthought, "if there is anything left of either of us by then."

When it is dark we go into town. Alcohol releases the tensions of the past weeks and helps us forget.

"Let us make it a proper celebration tonight, sir," Jonny suggests.

It seems like a good idea: I feel the same and am ready to agree to anything. For once there will be no restraint.

I thump Jonny heartily on the back.

"Jonny, my lad, you are absolutely right. Tonight we shall make it a really wild party!"

We roll and zigzag through the streets, singing and shouting. Luckily it is dark. No one sees us, which is just as well.

Jonny knows a young widow living in town. We go up to her place. She has her girl friend come over. Then we drink and dance until our feet no longer support us.

Nothing matters now, except to get away from it all and to be able just for a little while to forget. . . .

I spend the night in a strange bed.

March 24, 1944

When I arrive out at the dispersal point this morning, I am greeted with a loud chorus: "Happy birthday to you!"

The Flight is lined up, having been fallen in under the Senior Engineer. I walk down the ranks and shake hands with each one of my men.

I have known them all for years: every face is familiar. I know that they like me, and I cannot help feeling rather proud of them. My aim has always been to create and develop a spirit of special unity and comradeship within the Flight. In this I have succeeded. We are all united by a single common ideal: "The Fifth!"

April 28, 1944

A steady stream of new pilots arrived on posting to us during recent weeks. With the exception of a Flight Sergeant who came from the Eastern Front, where he had been awarded the Iron Cross, they are all young NCOs without experience, posted to us directly upon completion of courses at training schools which are altogether inadequate for operational requirements.

In personal character and physique, however, they are an exceptionally fine bunch of carefully selected youngsters. I myself take them up for about 120 training flights. Two veteran combat pilots also give them instruction in blind flying. In addition, they receive advanced instruction in bombing and gunnery.

In the middle of April, Barran, our good old Methuselah, rejoins us after his discharge from hospital.

Brand-new aircraft arrive straight from the factory. They are equipped with supercharged engines and the new methane device. The latter is something which I myself tested. It makes it possible for us to obtain from the engine a power boost of as much as 40 per cent for several minutes in case of emergency. This power boost is obtained by the injection into the cylinders of a mixture of methyl alcohol and water.

A camera is also attached to my plane. Several extracts from my latest films appeared in the *"Deutschen Wochenschau"* *(German Weekly Review)* newsreels in movie theaters everywhere in Germany.

"The Fifth" is back!

From April 15 to 20, I was attached to the Experimental Station at Lechfeld, where I flew for the first time a jet aircraft, the ME 262. In an ordinary standard model in level flight I reached a speed of 580 miles per hour. One thousand of these planes are to be on operations before the end of the year. God help the Tommy and the Yank then!

A few weeks ago at Zwischenahn I watched Major Späthe fly a ME 163. In three minutes he had climbed to 25,000 feet. This plane is rumored to be capable of a speed of more than 750 miles per hour. As far back as 1941 it was already doing over 600 miles per hour.

Development of other new types goes ahead rapidly. The German aircraft production industry is certainly operating in high gear now.

On the other side of the picture, however, are the American bombs which day after day come raining down on the factories. Will they succeed in bringing German aircraft production to a standstill before the new models can be produced in quantity? The answer to that question will decide the outcome of the air war over the Reich: it has become a sort of murderous race against time. The outlook is dark.

Day after day the Eastern Front has to be withdrawn. Africa was written off in March: 120,000 German soldiers there became prisoners, all of them well-trained and experienced combat veterans. The situation in Italy has become critical. The Italians as allies are utterly useless and unreliable and have never been anything else.

In the west we must expect an American landing on the Continent. For several months the Squadron has been making preparations down to the last detail for "Operation Doctor Gustav Wilhelm." Every pilot has received extensive theoretical training in preparation for operations against landing craft and transports.

The press of a button at the first alarm is sufficient to set the entire vast organization in the west rolling into action.

This morning Major Specht is appointed Commanding Officer *(Geschwaderkommodore)* of No. 11 Fighter Wing. A few days ago he was awarded the Knight's Cross.

I am appointed to succeed him as Commanding Officer of the Second Squadron of No. 11 Fighter Wing (II/JG. 11). I am also advised of my accelerated promotion to the rank of Captain *(Hauptmann)*, owing to "bravery in the face of the enemy." At 23 years of age I seem to be for the moment the youngest Squadron Commander in the German Air Force.

Little Specht smiles as he shakes hands with me three times and congratulates me: one, on my promotion to Captain; two, on my appointment as Commanding Officer *(Kommandeur)*; and three—because Lilo has just presented me with our second daughter.

It is a marvelous day; the sun is shining, and the lowering clouds are still far away on the horizon.

April 29, 1944

"Concentrations of enemy aircraft in Dora-Dora!" Here we go again! The reorganized Squadron is ready for action.

Three Bomber Divisions are launching an offensive from the Great Yarmouth area. Our formations in Holland report strong fighter escorts. My orders are to engage the escorting fighters in combat with my Squadron, draw them off and keep them occupied. Other Squadrons of Focke-Wulfs are thus to be enabled to deal with the bombers effectively without interference.

1000 hours. "Stand by, the entire Squadron!"

I have a direct ground line from my aircraft to the control room at Division. Enemy situation reports are relayed to me all the time. They pass over Amsterdam . . . the south tip of Ijssel Bay . . . north of Deventer . . . crossing the Reich border . . . west of Rheine.

At 1100 hours the spearhead of the formation is over Rheine.

1104 hours. "Entire Squadron to take off; entire Squadron to take off!" The order booms forth from the loud-speakers across the field. Signal rockets and Very lights are sent up from the Flight dispersal points. Engines roar. We are off! The Flights rise from the field and circle to the left, closing in to make up a single compact Squadron formation.

I turn on the radio and contact base. "Heavy babies in sector Gustav-Quelle. Go to Hanni-eight-zero."

"Victor, victor," I acknowledge.

I continue climbing in a wide circle to the left up to the required operational altitude . . . 20,000 . . . 22,000 . . . 25,000 feet.

North and south of us other Squadrons are also climbing. They are mostly Focke-Wulfs.

"Heavy babies now in Gustav-Siegfried; Hanni-eight-zero."

"Victor, victor."

I have now reached 30,000 feet. The new superchargers are marvelous.

1130 hours. Off to the west and below I spot the first vapor trails. They are Lightnings. In a few minutes they are directly below, followed by the heavy bombers. These are strung out in an immense chain as far as the eye can reach. Thunderbolts and Mustangs wheel and spiral overhead and alongside.

Then our Focke-Wulfs sweep right into them. At once I peel off and dive into the Lightnings below. They spot us and swing round toward us to meet the attack. A pack of Thunderbolts, about 30 in all, also come wheeling in toward us from the south. This is exactly what I wanted.

The way is now clear for the Focke-Wulfs. The first of the Fortresses are already in flames. Major Moritz goes in to attack with his Squadron of in-fighters *(Rammjaeger)*.

Then we are in a madly milling dogfight. Our job is done; it is a case of every man for himself. I remain on the tail of a Lightning for several minutes. It flies like the devil himself, turning, diving, and climbing almost like a rocket. I am never able to fire more than a few pot shots.

Then a flight of Mustangs dives past. Tracers whistle close by my head. I pull back the stick with both hands, and the plane climbs steeply out of the way. My wingman, Sergeant Drühe, remains close to my tail.

Once again I have a chance to fire at a Lightning. My salvos register at last. Smoke billows out of the right engine. I have to break away, however. Glancing back, I see that I have *eight* Thunderbolts sitting on my tail. The enemy tracers again come whistling past my head.

Evidently my opponents are old hands at the game. I turn and dive and climb and roll and loop and spin. I use the methanol emergency booster, and try to get away in my favorite "corkscrew climb." In only a few seconds the bastards are right back on my tail. They keep on firing all the time. I do not know how they just miss me, but they do.

My wingman sticks to me like glue, either behind or alongside. I call him to "Stay right there!" whatever happens. "Victor, victor," he calmly replies.

In what I think could be a lucky break, I get a Yank in my sights. I open fire with all guns. The crate goes up in a steep climb. Then all his comrades are back again on my tail.

In spite of the freezing cold, sweat pours down my face. This kind of dogfight is hell. One moment I am thrust down into the seat in a tight turn; the next I am upside down, hanging in the safety harness with my head practically touching the canopy roof and the guts coming up into my mouth.

Every second seems like a lifetime.

The Focke-Wulfs have meanwhile done a good job. I have seen nearly 30 of the Fortresses go down in flames. But there are still several hundred more of the heavy bombers winging their way eastward undaunted. Berlin is in for another hot day.

My fuel indicator needle registers zero. The red light starts to flicker its warning. Ten more minutes only, and my tank will be empty. I go down in a tight spiral dive. The Thunderbolts break away.

Just above the clouds, at an altitude of 3,000 feet, I slowly level off. I estimate that I am probably somewhere in the vicinity of Brunswick or Hildesheim.

I look at my watch. Perhaps in another 45 minutes I shall

be over the bomber alley again. Perhaps then I shall be able to get a fat bomber in front of my guns. . . .

Overhead, the sky is still streaked with vapor trails, stamped with the imprint of that infernal dogfight. Suddenly the wingman beside me flicks his aircraft round and vanishes into the cloudbank.

What the hell. . . ?

In a flash I glance round, and then instinctively duck my head. There is a Thunderbolt sitting right on my tail, followed by seven more. All eight open fire. Their salvos slam into my plane. My right wing bursts into flames.

I spiral off to the left into the clouds. A shadow looms ahead: it is a Thunderbolt. I open fire. Its tail is soon in flames.

Now I can see the ground. I jettison the canopy and am ready to bail out. There is another rat-tat-tat sound of machine guns close to my ear and more hammer blows hit my flaming crate. That Thunderbolt is there again, not 100 feet behind me.

Damn! I will be chewed to mincemeat in his prop if I try to bail out now. I huddle down and crouch low in my seat, trying to make myself as small as possible. The armor plate at my back protects me from the otherwise fatal shots. Wings and fuselage are riddled. A large hole gapes beside my right leg. The flames are licking closer now: I can feel the heat.

Crash! The instrument panel flies into splinters in front of my eyes. Something strikes me on the head. Then my engine stops: not a drop of fuel left.

What chance have I now?

My forward speed, of course, rapidly decreases. This causes my opponent to overshoot and pass me. For a few seconds only he is in my sights; but it is a chance to take him with me. I press both triggers. I feel myself trembling all over from the nervous tension. If I can only take him with me!

My salvo scores a perfect bull's-eye right in the center of his fuselage. He pulls up his smoking plane in a steep climb. In a moment he is in flames. The canopy opens and the body of the pilot emerges.

The ground comes up with a rush. Too late for me to bail out now. I cross some large fields. Down goes the nose and the plane settles. The flames come up, reaching for my face. Earth flies into the air. There is a dull, heavy thud. The crate skids along in a cloud of dust, then digs its own grave in the soft earth. I throw up my arms to cover my face, and brace my legs against the rudder bar. It is all over in a split second. Something crashes with stunning force on to my head.

So this must be the end! It is my last thought before losing consciousness. . . .

I have no recollection of getting clear of that burning wreck, but I suppose I must have done so. Coherent thought is beyond me: there is only that dreadful pain in my head. I remember bullets flying past my ears as the ammunition explodes. I stumble and fall, but somehow stagger to my feet again. My one idea is to get away before the final explosion. The bright flames consuming my aircraft contrast vividly against the dark smoke pall rising into the sky behind it.

A second wreck is burning only a few hundred yards away. Dimly I realize that it must be my Yank. If only the pain would stop! My head! my head!—I hold it in both hands and sink to my knees. The world spins crazily in front of my eyes. I am overcome by recurrent nausea, until only the taste of green bile remains.

I finally roll into a shallow ditch and pass out again. I am at the end of my tether. . . .

When next I recover consciousness, I become aware of a man standing motionless and staring down at me. He is as tall as a young tree—an American!

I try to sit up on the edge of the ditch. The big fellow sits down beside me. At first neither of us speak. It is all I can do to prop my elbows on my knees and hold my splitting head in my hands. Then the Yank offers me a cigarette. I thank him and refuse, at the same time offering him one of mine. He also refuses; so we both light up our own.

"Was that you flying the Messerschmitt?"

"Yes," I answer in my rusty English.

"You wounded?"

"Feels like it."

"The back of your head is bleeding."

I can feel the blood trickling down my neck.

The Yank continues: "Did you really shoot me **down?**"

"Yes."

"But I don't see how you could! Your kite was a mass of flames."

"Don't I know it!"

The tall American explains how he spotted me above the clouds and went down after me with his men. "It sure seemed like a bit of luck," he added.

I ask him in turn: "What was your idea in getting out in front of me when my engine died?"

"Too much forward speed. Besides, it never occurred to me that you would still be firing."

"That is where you made your mistake."

He laughs. "Guess I'm not the first you bagged, am I?"

"No; you are my twenty-sixth."

The American tells me that he has shot down 17 Germans. In a few more days he was due to go home. He notices the ring on my finger and asks if I am married.

"Yes; and I have two little children." I show him a picture of Lilo and Ingrid.

"Very nice," he remarks, nodding in appreciation, "very, very nice indeed."

I am glad he likes them.

He also is married. His wife over there will have to wait for him in vain now. Rather anxiously, the big fellow asks what is going to happen to him.

I explain that he will be sent to a special POW camp for American airmen. "Are you an officer?"

"Yes; a Captain."

"In that case you will go to a camp for officers. You will be well treated. Our prisoners are just as well treated as yours."

We have a friendly chat for about half an hour. He seems like a decent fellow. There is no suggestion of hatred between us, nor any reason for it. We have too much in common. We are both pilots, and we have both just narrowly escaped death.

A squad of soldiers from a nearby searchlight battery arrives, and we are covered with raised rifles.

"Put away that damned artillery, you clods," I call over to them.

On the highway there is a truck waiting for us. Six Yanks from a Fortress are huddled in the back. They look rather gloomy. My Captain and I sit beside them. Although feeling like death myself, I try to cheer up the party with a few jokes.

On the road we collect more Yanks who were shot down. One of them is badly wounded in the leg. I see that our men lift him up carefully into the truck.

We are driven to the Brunswick Airfield at Broitzum.

There I say farewell to my fellow-sufferers, and we all shake hands.

"Good luck!"

"All the best!"

"*Auf Wiedersehen!*"

One hour later Barran flies over and collects me in an Arado. The Squadron all returned without further casualties. I am the only one who was caught.

Later, in the operations room, I collapse, unconscious again. They first take me to my quarters, where I develop a raging fever. During the night I am admitted to the hospital.

7

Several grim weeks have passed. The doctors found a fracture at the base of my skull. A dangerous brain hemorrhage followed, and then I had a complete nervous breakdown. For several days I could not utter a word. Even now my speech is not yet quite normal. My memory has been affected and I am still very jittery. They want to send me to a psychiatric hospital. I refuse to go; that really would send me crazy.

A few days ago the Allies landed in Normandy. My Squadron has been moved to the invasion sector under the command of my old comrade, Captain Krupinsky.

I telephone Second Fighter Division and request to be returned to operation duties forthwith. The General refuses: "Knoke, your first duty now is to get yourself fit. You are not yet equal to going into the invasion sector. I am not going to let you commit suicide by sending you back on operations just now. You ought to think of your family."

Yesterday I took a thorough medical examination at the Air Force hospital. The result was shattering: I am totally unfit for flying duties.

In deep anxiety I have been following the latest developments at the front.

The Russians advance inexorably closer to the German border in the east. Our armies in Russia are exhausted. The Divisions there have been in action without respite since 1941. Reinforcements which were intended to strengthen them have had to be diverted for the defense of the West.

July 20, 1944

Attempt to assassinate the Führer!

A wave of intense indignation sweeps through the German people. What could be the motive of the conspirators? The ordinary German fighting soldiers regard the unsuccessful revolt as treason of the most infamous kind.

We know only too well the effect of the Nazi regime, with its follies and excesses. We see that conditions in the Reich leave much to be desired. The elimination of this unsatisfactory state of affairs will be the first duty of the German fighting soldiers as soon as the war is over.

First things first, however. The immediate problem is Germany itself; for the very existence of the Reich is at stake.

August 6, 1944

For the past two months I have been up in the mountains beside Lake Tegernsee. My wounds are healed, and I have made a remarkable recovery.

I cannot help thinking of my comrades, at this time of difficulty and danger. I am almost ashamed of myself to be living up here like a lord in a mansion.

Today I learned that Jonny Fest has now also been killed in action, shot down by Thunderbolts. This is a terrible shock.

August 10, 1944

A two-day medical board examination has resulted in another disappointment. I am not fit for flying duties.

My medical documents and records, including the findings of the board, are handed to me with instructions to give them to the Medical Officer of the new unit to which I shall be posted.

I shall forget to do so. Loss of memory has some compensations.

August 11, 1944

My old Squadron is back at Wunsdorf for a short rest. I travel there and visit my old friend Krupinsky.

Later I report by telephone to Division as having been discharged fit, and receive orders to proceed to France with the Squadron for the purpose of taking over the command of the Third Squadron of No. 1 Fighter Wing.

August 12, 1944

We are transferred to Wiesbaden in the evening with 74 aircraft.

Krupinsky has to bail out en route when his aircraft catches fire. He is injured and admitted to hospital, and so I take over temporary command of the Squadron following our landing at Wiesbaden.

August 13, 1944

The movement order for us to transfer to the front arrives very late in the evening. It is almost dark when we appear over the rolled-down cornfield which is to serve as our makeshift landing ground.

Senior Lieutenant Kirchner crashes into a telephone pole in the dark and is killed. It is a miracle that the other aircraft succeed in landing safely. A huge cloud of dust rises every time one of them touches down.

During the night I am driven over to the Third Squadron of No. 1 Fighter Wing (III/JG. 1), to take command of my new "gang."

To my astonishment I discover that I am to replace Captain Woitke, my first operational Commanding Officer in the war. We shake hands when I report, and it is as if the years suddenly roll back and I am once again the young and inexperienced pilot reporting to him on my first operational posting to the Second Squadron of No. 52 Fighter Wing.

Woitke laughs at my surprised face. I took it for granted that this old soldier, with all his seniority and experience, would by now have been at least a Lieutenant Colonel.

He was shot down a few days ago and wounded. The already gigantic appearance of the man is increased by his chest and left arm being in a cast. It seems that the stories of his continual indulgence in liquor have not been viewed favorably at the Air Force High Command.

During the night he hands over command of the Squadron.

August 14, 1944

For my first mission I go up early in the morning with a wingman.

Over Rennes we encounter six Thunderbolts. By emerging from a cloud at the right moment I am able to shoot down one of them. It explodes in mid-air. I immediately withdraw into the cloud again and head back for base. On a road below I observe a procession of jeeps with small trailers. We dive and strafe them. One of the jeeps bursts into flames and goes careening down an embankment.

During the afternoon we fly two more missions, escorting our fighter-bombers in attacks on the American positions northwest of Rennes.

August 15, 1944

The weather is unbearably hot and sultry.

Once more we fly as escort to our fighter-bombers. In a dogfight I bring my score up to 28 by shooting down another Thunderbolt.

Altogether six missions are flown today.

August 16, 1944

Spitfires come over in a dawn attack on our airstrip and strafe the dispersal area of No. 10 Flight, but without causing much damage. I take off in pursuit at the head of a Section, and shoot down a Spitfire over Etampes.

Two more missions are flown during the day, but without any noteworthy success. We attack and strafe the Allied transport columns.

August 17, 1944

At 1000 hours an intruder appears on reconnaissance over the airstrip, at the very moment when some of our aircraft are landing. That bastard is going to set his bomber comrades on to us!

Sure enough, eight fighter-bombers appear an hour later and strafe the dispersal areas, destroying one of our aircraft. Before the dust has time to settle, I am out of my camouflaged shelter and take off in pursuit to intercept the raiders.

Instead of catching them, I get a Lightning which is flying alone, apparently on reconnaissance. Over the village of Auxonette I manage to shoot it down.

In the evening the runway suddenly erupts in geysers of earth, just when we return from operations against the advancing American tanks and are about to land. Then I notice, shimmering in the hot sky overhead, a pack of some 12 Marauders. We attack them, although fuel is running dangerously low. Three are shot down by my men; a fourth is credited to me.

We are obliged to land at Bretigny, because of the number of deep crater pits in our runway.

During the night the Squadron is moved to Marolles.

August 18, 1944

From above Etampes the Americans push forward to the Seine, north of Paris.

The Wing is ordered to move to Vailly, east of Soissons. An advance ground party is immediately organized with fast tractors to receive the formations of aircraft as they arrive.

With my 40 aircraft I strafe the enemy supply columns near Avrenges, in conjunction with the other Squadrons which constitute the Wing. Over Lisieux I manage to shoot down a Mustang. Five minutes later a second Mustang goes down before my guns.

August 19, 1944

There was once a time when I used to count the years of my life by the summers.

It is different now. This summer is more like a nightmare from which there is no awakening. The heat is oppressive this August in France, as Death reaps his gory harvest: every day I am dodging the strokes of the scythe.

The worst part of it is the waiting—waiting for the scythe to catch me as it has caught the others, waiting while the hours drag into days, waiting as one day follows inexorably after another. Death itself I do not fear; for it is quick. I have escaped it often enough in the past to know that. It is the

an umbrella, together with a cordon of concentrated flak to protect the crossing.

During six missions in this sector yesterday the Squadron lost 12 aircraft. We are finished.

This morning the Squadron serviceability report lists only four aircraft as operational. Two others with badly twisted fuselages are capable of nonoperational flying only. They are such battered old crates that I am not going to be responsible for sending any of my men into combat in them.

So at 0600 hours there is a telephone call from the Chief Staff Officer at Corps Headquarters. He gives me a furious reprimand.

"This morning you reported only four aircraft available for operations. I have just learned that you can still fly six. Are you crazy? Do you realize the seriousness of the situation? It is nothing but sabotage; and I am not going to tolerate it. Every one of your aircraft is to fly. That is an order!"

He is bellowing like a bull. I have never been reprimanded like this since I finished my basic training as an Air Force recruit. I am so furious that I can hardly control my rage. Why should I have to listen to that arrogant ape? He even has the nerve to accuse *me* of sabotage! Chairborne strategists and heroes of the Staff make me sick. They know nothing of the problems at the front which we are up against, and they care even less.

I decide to fly one of the worn-out crates myself, and let my wingman, Corporal Döring, take the other. According to the operation orders, we are to take off at 0800 hours and rendezvous with the other Squadrons of the Wing over Soissons. I am then to take over command of the entire fighter formation.

Two minutes before zero hour the engines are started. We roll out from the camouflaged bushes and turn into wind.

There is no runway, only a length of soft field. My aircraft lumbers along, gathering flying speed with difficulty, and it is all I can do to coax the old crate into the air in time to clear the trees at the far end of the field.

Döring tries to climb too soon and stalls. His left wing drops and he plunges to crash into the trees. Flames belch forth. Döring is instantly killed—and then we are five.

The order from the Chief Staff Officer at Corps is worse than insanity; it amounts to nothing less than murder!

Base reports by radio to advise me that the other Squadrons are unable to leave the ground, because their fields are being strafed by enemy fighter-bombers.

"Go to sector Siegfried-Gustav."

North of Soissons lies the little town of Tergnier. It is a large railway junction at the point where the Somme Canal meets the River Oise. As a conspicuous landmark it is visible from a great distance. Above it, the Third Squadron of No. 1 Fighter Wing now fights its last air battle against the Americans over French territory.

We encounter more than 60 Thunderbolts and Mustangs in this area. There can be no escape: it is the end. All that remains is for me to give the order to attack. Thus at least a moral victory can still be claimed by my men and myself.

Base still tries to give me orders. I turn off the radio; to hell with them now!

My aircraft cannot climb above 10,000 feet. It is very slow and unresponsive. I feel certain that this is its last flight.

The battle does not last for more than a few minutes. Corporal Wagner is the first to be shot down; he does not escape from his flaming aircraft.

Then I see another aircraft on fire, and Flight Sergeant Freigang bails out. His wingman goes down in flames a few moments later.

That leaves only my wingman, Sergeant Ickes, and myself. For us there can be no way out. If this is to be the end, I can only sell my life as dearly as possible. If I ram one of the Yanks I shall be able to take him with me.

Tracers converge on us from all sides. Bullets slam my aircraft like hailstones, and it gradually loses forward speed. Ickes remains close beside me. I keep on circling in as tight a turn as possible. A Mustang gets on to my tail. I am unable to shake it off. My plane is too sluggish, as if it felt too tired to fly any farther. More bullets come slamming into the fuselage behind my head.

With a last burst of power from the engine I pull the aircraft up in a climb, half roll on to the side, and cut the throttle. The Mustang on my tail has not anticipated this. It shoots past, and now it is in front of me and a little below. I distinctly see the face of the pilot as he turns his head to look for me. Too late, he attempts to escape by diving. I am on him now. I can at least ram him if I cannot shoot him down. I feel icy cold.

The gap closes rapidly: we are only a few feet apart. My salvos slam into the fuselage: I am aiming for the pilot. His engine bursts into flames. We shall go down together!

There is a violent jolt at the first impact. I see my right wing fold and break away. In a split second I jettison the canopy and am out of the seat. There is a fierce blast of flame as I am thrown clear, while Messerschmitt and Thunderbolt are fused together in a single ball of fire.

A few moments later my parachute mushrooms overhead. Six to 800 feet away and a little higher up there is another open parachute. Ickes.

Overhead and all around us the Americans continue to thunder, circling and milling around like mad. It is a few minutes before it dawns on them that by this time not a single Messerschmitt is left in the sky.

I come down to land in a forest clearing. I have no idea whether I am on the German side or behind the enemy lines. Therefore, I start by hiding in the dense undergrowth.

Overhead, the Americans fly away to the west.

It is wonderful to be able to relax. I light a cigarette and lie back on the parachute shrouds, gratefully inhaling the soothing smoke.

As a precautionary measure, I remove the rank badges from my shoulders and stuff the German Gold Cross into my pocket.

I happen to be wearing an ordinary leather flying-jacket, a dark blue silk sports shirt, rather faded trousers, and black walking shoes. The whole effect is so un-Prussian that no one will recognize me immediately as a German.

My caution very soon proves justified.

About 15 minutes after my descent I notice four French civilians at the other end of the clearing. They gesticulate wildly as they talk. With my school French I am able to understand that they must be looking for me. Each one of them wants to search in a different place. I gather that they are under the impression that the parachutist is an American. All four carry arms. Evidently they are underground terrorists of the French Resistance.

I grope for the pistol hidden under my bulky leather jacket.

The four start combing the bushy undergrowth. Discovery is inevitable, sooner or later, so I decide to go out to meet them.

All four look surprised to see me. Four Tommy guns swing round to cover me. Now is the time for me to keep calm and clever. The French have a bitter hatred for us Germans, from the bottom of their temperamental souls. Not that I blame them; no doubt I should feel the same in their place. But if the bastards ever guess that I am German it will mean a bellyful of lead.

So I walk up coolly and in the friendliest possible manner greet them in English: "Hello, boys!"

The stern faces of the bandits gradually relax into smiles. They take me for a Yank.

In my best American accent I then proceed to ask them in very broken French to help me find my "comrades": "*Voulez-vous aider moi trouver mes camarades?*"

They immediately explain the position to me. An American armored unit with Sherman tanks is a little over a mile away. We must be very cautious, however, as the place is still swarming with the lousy Boches. Fighting is going on all round us. In fact I can now hear for the first time the distant gunfire.

The tallest of the Frenchmen—a thoroughly repulsive-looking type—carries a German Tommy gun. I do not like the look of him at all. He remains in the background, suspiciously quiet. Does he doubt that I am what I appear to be?

We make our way through the dense forest until we come to a railway embankment.

There is a sudden chattering from a German machine gun; it sounds like an MG 45 and is quite close. The three Frenchies in front drop flat on their faces. The tall bandit remains standing close to me; evidently he is not going to let me out of his sight. From the other side of the railway comes the grinding clatter of heavy tank engines.

I ask where the line goes.

"*Vers Amiens.*"

Amiens! ! ? Did I really drift so far west during the dog-fight? The city has been in American hands for some time. Damn! I have no desire to spend the rest of the war sitting in a prison camp somewhere in the U.S.A.

The nearest town, I learn, is Nesle. Then the Somme Canal must be somewhere to the north. According to the early morning intelligence reports, it is still being held by our forces. I shall have to head north. But how am I going to get rid of those blasted Frenchies?

More heavy gunfire is heard. The sound comes from the west. The Frenchmen cautiously cross the tracks and wave to me to follow them. The big fellow stays on my tail with his Tommy gun, otherwise I would be able to bolt back into the forest and then make my way round to the north.

A few hundred yards farther on we come to a highway. It cuts across the landscape, straight as an arrow, and is visible for miles.

The chattering of several machine guns is again heard off to the left. The first three Frenchmen cautiously cross the road. The big fellow takes two or three paces after them, then turns toward me. Our eyes meet. I can tell that he recognizes me. I must be off! There will be no second chance to break away; it must be now or never.

I dash back toward the forest. Then the big fellow is coming after me before his comrades realize what is happening. He lifts his Tommy gun and starts firing. I drop behind a bank of earth. Bullets thud into the ground all round me.

The bandit empties his clip. He must take his eyes off the target long enough to insert a new one. There is just enough time to draw my pistol and snap up the safety catch. I leap at the big fellow, who is raising his Tommy gun again, and fire once. It is enough. He goes down with a bullet in the head.

I take his Tommy gun. "Sorry, my friend, but he who hits first lives longest."

Panting, I struggle through the dense undergrowth. Twigs

and branches lash at my face. The other three Frenchmen are left behind.

Fifteen minutes later I run into a German patrol. They are soldiers from an armored unit.

At Chauny the Commanding Officer of a German Air Force unit lets me have his car. It is late at night when I arrive back at my airstrip.

I have taken an old French château for my headquarters. My Adjutant, Captain Marschall, the Medical Officer, the Engineering Officer, and Captain Wessels, who commands the Headquarters Company, are still sitting in the dining room. They welcome my return with loud cheers. Their faces become grave as I tell them of the fate of our comrades.

Before I have finished the story I receive a telephone call from the Wing. The Commanding Officer is on the line. His news is far from pleasant.

Enemy tanks have made an unexpected forward thrust from Château-Thierry toward Soissons and Fismes. Heavy fighting is now raging round both towns. One of the American armored spearheads is only a few miles south of our field. Other enemy forces have cut us off in the east. In the north the enemy pressure is heavy on Laon.

If the Allied advance cannot be checked in the Laon sector, then we really shall be in the soup. I have all Flights alerted immediately, and give orders for a general evacuation of the Squadron to a field near the village of Beaumont in Belgium. A few days ago I was there on a reconnaissance to find a landing strip in anticipation of a possible withdrawal. We have a small advance party there already.

August 29, 1944

We work hard all through the night.

Six hours after the evacuation orders the airstrip is clear.

Flight dispersal bases, squadron operations room, and head-quarters, mobile repair workshops—everything is dismantled. Already 128 vehicles are on the move for Beaumont, with every piece of equipment and the Squadron ground staff of more than 600 men.

I have given orders for every vehicle to proceed individually, and not in convoy, in order to reduce the danger of bombing and strafing from the air. The few roads which are not blocked by the enemy are jammed for miles by vehicles retreating in convoy.

The French civilian residents of our château have put on their Sunday clothes, and prepare to welcome the American liberators with baskets of fruit and flowers. They are horrified when the Sherman tanks begin to bombard the building. Even as a pretty little French girl, beautifully dressed in her Sunday best, is serving me an early breakfast, a mortar shell crashes into the château tower.

The enemy has now reached the next village, little more than a mile to the south. Only an hour ago No. 8 Flight had its orderly room there. Along the road between there and our quarters, our Infantry on the north bank of the Aisne is slowly retreating under cover of the tanks in the direction of Vailly.

Out on the airstrip the last length of cable from the field-telephone system is rolled up. It is loaded on to the last of the Squadron vehicles, a Signals jeep, which then drives off to cross the bridge over the Aisne.

On the high ground north of Vailly I pause to take a last look back at our abandoned airstrip. Even as I watch, the bridges behind us are demolished in a series of terrific detonations.

My fast Ford V-8 is good for threading through the congested traffic cluttering up the only road still open to Laon.

The city itself was bombed by several waves of Marauders scarcely an hour before we arrive, and is now ablaze from end to end. The approaches to the city are blocked by German transport convoys under continual enemy bombing and strafing. They are exposed and practically defenseless against attack, and burning vehicles are everywhere.

For several hours I shelter in a thicket off the main highway, waiting for the attacks to end. It is dark before we are able to drive through the blazing streets of Laon.

One problem which causes me grave concern is: What has become of my men?

Driving at night with dimmed headlights requires intense concentration. My driver and I take turns at the wheel. Never-ending convoys still keep jamming the road. Vehicles keep breaking down and stopping. The French Resistance fighters have strewn the highway with nails and small contact mines. I am glad that I ordered brushes to be attached to my vehicles in front of the wheels, to protect them from punctures.

By dawn I feel exhausted. The fatigue and nervous strain of the past 48 hours begin to tell. I drive the car off the highway into the shelter of a wood. In a very few minutes I am sleeping the sleep of the dead.

September 1, 1944

Every last vehicle belonging to the Squadron has reached Beaumont. Despite continual bombing and strafing attacks by day and terrorist activities by the French Resistance at night, not a single one of them is lost.

I am deeply shocked, both by the reports I receive on the deteriorating situation and by what I have seen with my own eyes during the last two days on the French highways.

It seems to be impossible to organize effective opposition to the enemy advance anywhere. A few of the armed SS and paratroop units still fight on desperately. Generally speaking, however, our armies suffer from lack of morale in combat. I am sick with disgust at having to watch our occupation forces pack up without any thought of resistance after years of being stationed in France. Personal safety seems to be all that matters to the civil administration and military government staffs. The retreat has degenerated into a cowardly, panicky rout, in which contact with the enemy has to be avoided at any cost. For years the officers and administrative officials of these units have been enjoying a life of parasitic luxury in France. All conception of fundamental military duty is forgotten. Bag and baggage, they clutter up the highways. Their vehicles are loaded with crates full of personal provisions and loot. Often their French girl friends travel with them to share in the spoils.

If we should lose this campaign, the conduct of the French women must bear a major share of the responsibility. Nights of passion and debauchery have undermined the morale of our officers and soldiers. They are no longer ready to sacrifice their lives to the glory of the Fatherland, thanks to the enthusiastic collaboration of those amateur and professional harlots.

If I were the Commander-in-Chief, I would clean up the mess in short order with a few general-courts-martial. That much at least we owe to the German soldiers who after years are still heroically fighting in the east.

The destiny of my Squadron is still undecided. For the present I have orders to construct another airstrip near Manches. I have approximately 1,000 soldiers and another 1,000 Belgian civilian laborers on the job.

September 10, 1944

No replacement pilots or aircraft have yet arrived.

A few days ago the Squadron was transferred to the Westerwald. I have flown on several operations together with the Headquarters Flight of the Wing. Dogfights with enemy fighter-bombers have enabled me to add to my steadily rising score.

Here in the Reich the situation has become completely chaotic, ever since Himmler, the Reich Leader of the SS, took over the command of all the Reserve Forces. It would seem that the Führer is transferring the command of the armed services from their own military leaders to his political party bosses. The reputation which Hitler established for himself at the beginning of the war as "the greatest military genius the world has ever seen" is slowly but surely evaporating. He would do better to leave to his experienced generals the business of conducting the war.

A few days ago I was present at a conference with General Galland, Chief of the Fighter Command. There is a possibility that my Squadron is to be disbanded altogether, owing to the extraordinary difficulty of bringing it back up to strength again. Production in our aircraft industry is being seriously impeded by Allied air attacks. Almost every hydrogenation factory has been destroyed, and the fuel shortage has become a matter of very grave concern.

Furthermore, a major stumbling block to the rebuilding of my Squadron seems to be the personnel problem. The vast majority of experienced fighter pilots have been either killed or wounded.

East and west, our fronts are withdrawn a little farther every day. We are still waiting for the new "secret weapon."

We fighter pilots in particular are anxiously awaiting the

appearance of jet aircraft on operations. Following an idiotic order given by Hitler a few weeks ago, the first jets to come off the assembly line are to be used only for purposes of "reprisal" (*Vergeltungswaffe*).

Hitler angrily rejects the protests which are made by all the fighter unit Commanding Officers, Galland, and even Göring. We are forbidden to so much as discuss the possibility of effectively using jets on operations.

The German Fighter Command is slowly bleeding to death in defense of the Reich; our cities and factories are being razed to the ground practically without opposition with deadly precision by the British and Americans. And the only idea Hitler can think of is "reprisal"!

If we could only have one or two Wings operating with the new ME 262s, there would still be a good chance for the German Fighter Command to save the situation. Otherwise the war in the air will be lost.

October 2, 1944

Two days ago I was attached to the Eighth Fighter Division. My Squadron is transferred to the Danube River above Vienna. Here I am to receive my replacement pilots and aircraft before being sent on operations in the Hungarian sector.

I had a happy reunion this morning. The Senior General Staff Officer at Division took me round the Headquarters to introduce me to the heads of the various branches. In the Intelligence Section whom should I encounter but Senior Lieutenant Günter Gerhard! I can scarcely believe my eyes; for this is my old friend whom I heard reported killed more than two years ago. Günter had also been informed that I had gone down in the great fighter graveyard of the west.

This was one of the happiest surprises of the war for me.

At my request, Günter is immediately posted to my Squadron, to replace Captain Marschall as my Adjutant. My old friend is delighted also to exchange a rather dreary existence on the staff at Headquarters for the clean atmosphere of an operational unit.

October 7, 1944

During the past few days there has been a steady flow of replacement pilots arriving on posting to report to me at my operations room. Some old, familiar faces are among them, men returning to active duty after recovering from wounds. Several of them are former bomber pilots, whose units have been disbanded.

Our aircraft are due to arrive during the next few days. I can only keep my fingers crossed and hope that at last they will be jets.

October 9, 1944

Today shatters all my hopes for future operations.

Shortly after midnight I receive orders by telephone to transfer to Anklam in North Germany. I myself am to proceed there in advance by road and report at a conference of the Commanding Officers of fighter units summoned by Reich Marshal Göring.

After drafting the necessary movement orders for the Squadron, I set off with Senior Lieutenant Gerhard and a driver by car at 0300 hours. We have 36 hours in which to make the journey, via Prague, Dresden, and Berlin, to Anklam. We carry all the fuel we need in cans stowed in the back of the car, since we cannot be certain of obtaining any en route.

In the afternoon around 1600 hours we stop for a short rest

and a cup of coffee at an inn in a Czech village. Refreshed, I take a turn at the wheel when we resume the journey. We have not gone half a mile, when the car is rocked by an explosion. The steering broken, we crash out of control into the parapet of a bridge. Gerhard beside me is thrown through the windshield and breaks a leg. The driver in the back succeeds in getting clear of the wreck and then collapses unconscious. I myself am pinned in my seat behind the wheel. The explosion wounded me; there are flying splinters embedded in my legs; blood comes oozing out of my boots. In desperation I try to drag myself clear. The noise of a car approaching is suddenly drowned by that of a second explosion. Then there is a terrific jolt, and a blazing Volkswagen crashes into my car, rebounds from the impact, skids across the road, and hurtles down a steep embankment on the other side. By making frantic efforts I eventually manage to drag myself out of the wreck.

My left knee is shattered, and so is my right pelvis. Lying on my back, I painfully inch my way on my elbows to the ditch by the roadside.

Two hours pass before we are finally picked up by men from an SS unit. The driver of the second vehicle is dead. Destruction of both vehicles is found to have been caused by means of limpet mines. It is a case of sabotage, committed by the Czech terrorist underground movement.

During the night we are taken to the Air Force hospital in Prague, where an immediate operation is found necessary for Günter and myself. My left leg has become swollen and discolored. The operating surgeon at first wants to amputate, because he can see no hope of saving it. I am in utter despair.

I have no desire to spend the remainder of my life as a cripple. It takes two and a half hours of working on my knee before they finally get it more or less patched up. Both legs are placed in splints, and then at last I am brought into a ward where Günter is lying with a leg in splints also, together with a number of other seriously wounded cases.

I get one of the nursing sisters to bring me my kit. I take out a bottle of brandy, which Günter and I empty in a few minutes.

And so this one night I feel no pain!

December 3, 1944

For eight weeks—eight long weeks, eight endless weeks—I have been lying in a cast, unable to move. Günter lies in the next bed. Days of monotony are varied only by nights of pain.

The serious wounds in my left knee have healed well. The right leg, however, is permanently crippled. I shall have to resign myself to the fact.

The doctor has promised to let me get up soon. Tomorrow morning the cast is to come off.

December 4, 1944

Early this morning they remove the cast.

Both my legs have become terribly thin. The right knee is still very stiff. I am so weak that I can scarcely sit up in bed. I want to get out of bed, to see if I can stand, to see if I can walk at all. But every time I try to set foot on the floor I am overcome by dizziness.

December 7, 1944

Two days ago I took my first steps on crutches round the ward. Yesterday I ventured out into the corridor.

Today I shall try to go out for a short walk beside the

Moldau River. I am determined to walk again. Even if it means learning from the beginning like a little child, I am still going to do it.

December 10, 1944

Every day I cover a little more ground on my outings. With the help of one of the nursing sisters I got as far as the theater. It is only a ten-minute walk for a fit person, but it took me more than an hour. My hands are covered with sores and blisters, but I am making decided progress.

December 12, 1944

I have been sent to a resort in the Austrian Alps for radium-bath treatment. The stiffness in the left knee is gradually disappearing. The right leg is still useless, however; it dangles from the injured hip, and will always remain more than two inches shorter than the other.

I spend hours taking long and tiring walks on crutches through the snow. Every day I have a hot radium bath, which is supposed to have a stimulating effect on muscles and joints.

December 16, 1944

The war news is grave. I can follow the enemy advances in both east and west on my maps. I have come to the conclusion that victory can no longer be achieved.

I do not believe that the war can come to a decisive conclusion, or that there will be any real victors. The only true measure of victory is lasting peace. I do not see how there can ever be lasting peace in the world as long as bolshevism continues to exist. It will have to go on one day to conquer the world, according to the Communist theories of world revolution. The price to be paid for a peace of that sort is the enslavement of every nation and all mankind.

December 19, 1944

Lilo has succeeded in arranging my transfer to the Navy hospital at Sanderbusch *(later to be taken over by the Canadian Army as No. 7 Canadian General Hospital)*, only a few miles from Jever. There we have a charming little house, which Lilo has made into a real home. There she is now waiting for me with our two children. We want to be together in whatever may happen during the difficult last days of the war.

December 21, 1944

I set off on crutches for my loved ones. All that matters to me is to get home. I am out of the war now, a cripple.

Salzburg has been heavily bombed just before my train arrives. We are transferred to trucks—20 of the more serious wound cases—and driven past the city to the next railway station.

It is a bitterly cold night when we arrive at Rosenheim, where we have to wait for a connection to Munich. Down come more bombs, and the railway station is destroyed. Thousands of people flee in panic as the bombs whine through the air. We who are too seriously wounded to run lie flat between the tracks, hugging the ground until the storm of metal has passed. Then we huddle together and freeze until the first train arrives several hours later.

At Munich the east station is on fire when we arrive. The British have been bombing that city also. Nursing sisters from the Red Cross help me when I am unable to walk any farther by myself. My comrades remain in Munich and go to hospital there.

The train takes seven hours to cover the journey to Augsburg. Under normal conditions it takes the inside of one hour only. All along the line the bombing during the night has torn up the permanent way.

At Augsburg station I am taken to a hut put up by the Red Cross. I cannot keep going. I am dead tired: I just want to close my eyes and sleep . . . sleep . . . sleep. . . .

December 22, 1944

They try to get me out of bed at noon. Fortresses are bombing the city, and they want to take me into an air-raid shelter. I throw them out and tell them to leave me alone. I still just want to sleep.

In the evening I leave on a troop train which is due to reach Hanover during the morning.

December 23, 1944

The strain of this journey has become rather too much for me. I ache in every joint and muscle. It is just as well that I find people everywhere who are kind and helpful. My crutches make me feel as helpless as a little child.

Railwaymen take me to the locomotive of a freight train leaving for Bremen. The driver's cabin is nice and warm. The engineer and fireman make me comfortable on a pile of awnings and sacking.

They are surprised to see my rank badges and decorations. They never knew that wounded front-line officers are capable of traveling in such a primitive fashion.

We talk about the war, about the destruction of cities and factories. The engineer lost his entire family with his home in the bombing of Bremen. The fireman lost his son-in-law, killed in Russia. Both feel, like myself, that we ought to make peace with the West in order to have a free hand in the East. Both are prepared to fight the Russians again, as they had as young men during the First World War.

A slow local passenger train finally brings me in to Jever at midnight. The Commanding Officer of the air station sends down his car to drive me home.

Standing in the darkness at the garden gate, I see Lilo come out of the house and run to me. I want to take her in my arms and hug her as I always did before, but this time I cannot do so. Both hands are needed for the crutches.

After kissing her, we go into the house together.

She speaks only once, and then her voice is trembling: "You walk so slowly," she says, "I had no idea it was so bad."

The living room is warm and comfortable. I am very, very tired. Tired of all the effort and discomfort of traveling, tired of all I have seen and heard and experienced, tired of war. I am happy, however, too. Happy to be home at last, happy that Lilo and I are together again.

Tomorrow is Christmas Eve. Tomorrow little Ingrid will be up and about, darting around with her blonde curls. She will be after me with innumerable questions: "Am I home now to stay; why was I away so long; why do I walk so slowly; why is there a war; why . . . why . . . why . . .?"

8

The End

Until the middle of January I am unable to leave the house. Snow and ice prevent me from reporting at the hospital.

I receive news from the Squadron that Captain Woitke resumed command after his recovery, but was killed in action a few days later. They send me my logbooks, together with official confirmation of my remaining victories and the news that I have been awarded the Knight's Cross (*Ritterkreuz des Eisernen Kreuzes*).

My logbooks contain records of nearly 2,000 flights, including more than 400 operational missions in the face of the enemy. I am credited with shooting down 52 aircraft. In distance I have flown more than half a million air miles. Shall I ever fly again?

On January 1, 1945, our Fighter Wings undertake their last large-scale air operation. British and American airfields in France and Belgium are successfully bombed and strafed. For many of my comrades this is indeed the last mission of all. It seems that nearly 500 German fighter pilots lose their lives. Major Specht is among those who do not return. I cannot help thinking of the New Year's party one year ago. The

209

great mission which the "little Commodore" was expecting
then came exactly one year later.

Having made this supreme effort, the German Fighter
Command, as such, for all practical purposes ceases to exist.
Only a few units survive for further action.

The advances of the enemy in both east and west have
meanwhile crossed the border into the Reich. Millions of
Germans in the east are fleeing before the approaching
Asiatic hordes. Words cannot begin to describe the horror
and misery of their plight.

My parents are among those who are forced to leave their
homes. My mother and sister reach me toward the end of
January. There is no trace anywhere of my father.

Round-the-clock bombing of our cities by the British and
Americans continues without respite. Hundreds of thousands
of people lose their lives in this way.

Heavy fighting still continues at the fronts. German soldiers fight desperately, defending every inch of soil in their
country to the very last. According to the most recent German casualty figures, it is estimated that we have lost
4,000,000 killed.

Day after day, even in such remote districts as here in
Friesia, rural peace is shattered by sirens wailing the alarm.
Again and again Lilo has to take the children and a few
suitcases to the shelter. A slit trench is dug for me in the
garden behind the house. I have never had much use for
concrete shelters; I like to see what is happening, and am
accustomed to doing so.

In March I report to the Commanding Officer of the air
station for ground duties. Despite my crutches, I am kept
on the move all day long, checking fields as possible landing
grounds for troop-carrying gliders, siting small local defense
posts, establishing a mobile flying-control organization.

We form a part of the Wilhelmshaven fortifications. The city has become a fortress and is to be defended to the last at all costs. The garrison will be supplied by air in the event of a blockade. I come under the garrison command for operational purposes, as Air Liaison Officer. There are some 40,000 naval personnel available for operations on land. All are inexperienced, and there are not enough arms for more than a small proportion of them.

As the weeks pass, I become more and more convinced of the futility of continued resistance in the west. Conservation of all our strength is necessary to halt the Russian advance into Europe. I know that in the event of an armistice in the west, millions of exhausted, discouraged, battle-weary German soldiers will take new heart and unite, hurling their last ounce of strength into the struggle against communism, to free their homes and save Europe from ultimate disaster.

I myself would have no hesitation in climbing into an aircraft to fly and fight again, until every Bolshevist in the world-conquering Asiatic horde has been driven out of the last corner of the German Fatherland.

This is not my idea alone; it is the desire of all the officers and soldiers with whom I have spoken in recent weeks. They and I look forward to the day when the Western Allies will come to realize that it is not Germany which is the real menace to their life and liberty, but Soviet Russia.

On our Heroes Memorial Day, March 11, 1945, I make the following entry in my diary:

> The war has become a standard by which the spirit of Germany may be measured, a spiritual line of division as it were. We recognize the distinction in peacetime between "good" and "evil." It is the brave now who are to be distinguished from the cowardly.
>
> The war also provides a chance for the brave to surpass

themselves. God has already endowed them with courage and strength. Although they may die, the heroism of their death must always remain immortal.

In this, the darkest hour of our beloved Fatherland, they are today remembered by the German people. I have only to close my eyes to see the comrades who flew and fell by my side in the fiercest actions of the war.

During the last two years I have become very lonely. Not many of my comrades have returned from what we ourselves called the "Great Fighter Graveyard." Often we were overwhelmed by the vast numerical superiority of the enemy; often we were gallantly defeated in air combat. Even in defeat, however, we can still remain victors in one sense— victors over ourselves, victors over the baser instincts which threatened to rob us of courage and faith.

Again and again we take off, always as a matter of course. Each time there are some who do not return; but there are never any questions or complaints. Those of us who survive have been wounded more than once. I myself, wounded five times, am now a cripple.

If it ever comes to a question of driving the Russians back to their forests and marshes and steppes, however, after an armistice with the West, I am more than willing to go out and fight again. There will be new comrades: together we may recapture the spirit of the past: together we may enter into and become a part of that tradition. There will be a smile when we first shake hands, and then a moment of seriousness as we remember our dead comrades. . . . Their spirit of cheerful recklessness will always remain, wherever there are fighter pilots together. With the task completed, and our homeland free once more, and the thunder of our engines echoing again through our beloved skies, then we can pay fitting tribute indeed to the memory of our heroes and our comrades.

Their death shall never be in vain.

The war is lost.

The war is lost . . . the war is lost. . . .

The words smash upon us like blows from a sledgehammer.

The German nation has collapsed in total, crushing defeat. The full significance of this is beyond my comprehension.

Hitler is dead. The Reich is overthrown and under enemy occupation. The once-proud German Army no longer exists: the surviving remnants are either in prison camps or roam the countryside as undisciplined gangs of hungry vagrants. The German soldier is dishonored; even the name of dead comrades is sullied.

Our world is reduced to rubble.

It is useless for us to trouble ourselves now over such academic questions as responsibility and war guilt.

The war is lost. It is enough that victory has gone to the stronger.

We are dazed by all the sensational disclosures and events which occur in rapid succession. For us, the road to the future must lead through poverty and want. Despotism without conscience has been revealed among the Nazis in the background around Hitler.

Disgusted and indignant, the German fighting soldiers and officers turn away from those whose brutal war crimes and atrocities are now exposed. These criminals, whose activities were as a rule restricted to the concentration camps and labor camps in rear defense areas, have dishonored the name of Germany. The atrocities committed under the sign of the swastika deserve the most severe punishment. The Allies ought to leave the criminals to the German fighting soldiers to bring to justice.

The war is lost. The armistice is signed. Does this mean that there will be peace?

Library of Congress Cataloging-in-Publication Data

Knoke, Heinz, 1921-
    I flew for the Führer : the story of a German fighter pilot
by Heinz Knoke ; translated by John Ewing ; with an introduction by
        E.R. Quesada.
            p.   cm. — (Wings of war)
Reprint. Originally published : New York: Henry Holt and Company, c1954.
        ISBN 0-8094-7966-4.   ISBN 0-8094-7967-2 (lib. bdg.)
    1. Knoke, Heinz, 1921- . 2. World War, 1939-1945—Aerial operations,
    German. 3. World War, 1939-1945—Personal narratives, German.
4. Fighter Pilots—Germany—Biography. 5. Germany. Luftwaffe—Biography.
                I. Title. II. Series.
    D787.K613 1989   940.54'4943'092—dc20 [B]   89-20332 CIP

Time-Life Books Inc. offers a wide range of fine music series,
including *Your Hit Parade*, original recordings from the '40s and '50s.
For subscription information, call 1-800-621-7026 or write Time-Life Music,
        P.O. Box C-32068, Richmond, Virginia 23261-2068.